THE GROWTH OF MILK WOOD

THE GROWTH OF
MILK WOOD

DOUGLAS CLEVERDON

WITH THE TEXTUAL VARIANTS OF
UNDER MILK WOOD
BY DYLAN THOMAS

LONDON
J. M. DENT & SONS LTD

Made in Great Britain
at the
Aldine Press · Letchworth · Herts
for
J. M. DENT & SONS LTD
Aldine House · Bedford Street · London
First published 1969
Reprinted 1969

SBN: 460 03828 1

FOR
NEST

CONTENTS

PREFACE

My primary qualification for attempting this study of the eleven versions of the text of *Under Milk Wood* is that, as a radio producer in the B.B.C., I was associated with the projected script from its early stages, played some part in encouraging Dylan Thomas to complete it, and finally produced it as a *Play for Voices* on the B.B.C. Third Programme on 25th January 1954. Subsequently I co-directed the original stage-production in 1956, first at the Edinburgh Festival and later in the West End, and ultimately directed the Broadway production in 1957, when I had the opportunity of meeting the two friends of Dylan Thomas who were most closely concerned with the New York stage-readings. *Under Milk Wood* has consequently been one of my chief avocations for a number of years; its importance as Dylan Thomas's major dramatic work justifies, I think, this extended treatment of the text.

The first part of this volume is concerned with the history of *Under Milk Wood*, and explains as fully as possible the reasons for successive elongations and revisions of the text. The second part consists of an Analysis of Textual Variants, which may be of interest not only to students and *aficionados* of Dylan Thomas but also to directors engaged in radio or stage productions. As both 'Dylan Thomas' and 'Thomas' seemed unduly formal, I have normally referred to him as Dylan [1] throughout the first part, and as D.T. in the second.

---

[1] As for the pronunciation of his Christian name, he is reported to have said: 'The English call me Dillan and the Welsh call me Dullan, but my friends call me —— [*unprintable*].'

My acknowledgments are due to the Antiquarian Department of the Times Book Shop Ltd, for their courtesy in allowing me to work on the manuscript of *Under Milk Wood* while it was in their possession: to the Trustees of the Dylan Thomas Copyrights and to Messrs J. M. Dent & Sons Ltd for permission to quote from Dylan Thomas's writings: to the British Broadcasting Corporation for the use of files and other material in their archives, and to the staff of the B.B.C. Reference Library and of the B.B.C. Historical Records for their unfailing helpfulness: to Mr David Higham, Miss Elizabeth Reitell, Mr Ruthven Todd, Mr Kenn Mileston and the editor of *Mademoiselle* for having provided me with scripts, or facsimiles of scripts, of various versions of *Under Milk Wood*: to Mrs Vernon Watkins, Mr Richard Hughes, Professor Ralph Maud, and (among B.B.C. producers) Aneirin Talfan Davies, Francis Dillon and R. D. Smith: to my wife for her meticulous typing of a complicated text and finally to Richard Burton, Diana Maddox, Donald Houston, Hugh Griffith, William Squire, Philip Burton, T. H. Evans and their fellow artists for their superb realization of the essence of *Under Milk Wood* on radio or on stage.

HISTORY OF THE TEXT

The text of *Under Milk Wood* has a chequered history.
The theme itself took a long time to germinate in Dylan
Thomas's imagination; and the process of construction
was hampered, particularly in the later stages, by com-
promises that were designed to adapt the work for such
differing purposes as radio feature, public reading, and
stage production.

The earliest specific reference to his conception of
Welsh village life as matter for a play has been recorded
by the novelist Richard Hughes. For many years Richard
Hughes and his wife Frances lived at Laugharne Castle,
an agreeable Georgian house built into the castle ruin,
and saw much of Dylan and Caitlin Thomas during their
various sojourns in Laugharne between 1936 and 1953.
It was on 18th December 1939 that Dylan, Frances
Hughes and the butcher played the leading parts in a one-
act farce, *The Devil among the Skins*, at a 'Laugharne
Entertainment', organized by Mrs Hughes in aid of the
Red Cross. Richard Hughes recalled the occasion in a
broadcast:

> Talking it over furiously round the fire in the small
> hours afterwards, we all agreed it was absurd to
> perform such utter rubbish to so noble an audience
> as the burgesses of Laugharne. Then Dylan had an
> idea: 'What Laugharne really needs is a play about
> well-known Laugharne characters—and get them all
> to play themselves.' After that the idea went through
> many metamorphoses before it was finally written.[1]

[1] Richard Hughes in *Portrait of Dylan Thomas*, B.B.C.
Third Programme, 9th November 1963.

It happened that, only a few weeks earlier, Dylan had read his poems in a B.B.C. feature programme, *The Modern Muse*, produced by D. G. Bridson from the B.B.C. studios in Manchester: in which W. H. Auden, Stephen Spender, Cecil Day Lewis and Louis MacNeice also read their poems. Wishing to broadcast some more poems, Dylan wrote, at Bridson's suggestion, to T. Rowland Hughes, a Welsh Regional producer in Cardiff. In his reply on 1st November 1939 Rowland Hughes wrote:

> I am, at the moment, trying to develop Verse Features, that is, long dramatic programmes in verse, and I am wondering whether you would like to try your hand at that sort of thing. You may have heard one by Wyn Griffith the other night . . .

Dylan promptly replied:

> I don't think I'd be able to do one of those long dramatic programmes in verse; I take such a long time writing anything, & the result, dramatically, is too often like a man shouting under the sea. But if you'd let me know a little more about these programmes—length, subjects unsuitable, etc.—I'd like to have a try. It sounds full of dramatic possibilities, if only I was . . .

Rowland Hughes replied, on 4th November:

> What I have in mind, of course, is something on the lines of Bridson's *March of the '45* or MacLeish's *The Fall of the City*, or my own programme for last St. David's Day . . .

These 'dramatic possibilities' may well have been at the back of Dylan's mind a fortnight later, when the idea of a play about the people of Laugharne occurred to him.

As early as 1932 or 1933 he had spoken to his socialist friend, Bert Trick, of his wish to write a sort of Welsh *Ulysses*; like *Under Milk Wood*, it would have been

2

contained within a framework of twenty-four hours. There is no doubt, of course, that *Under Milk Wood* derives ultimately from his own innate Welshness; but it is equally true that the stimulus was his feeling for Laugharne, 'this timeless, mild, beguiling island of a town', where he had been living now 'for fifteen years, or centuries'—so he described it in a programme on Laugharne that was broadcast, by a strange irony, on the day that he fell into his death coma.

His first visit to Laugharne was in 1934, when he spent Whitsuntide with the Welsh poet and novelist Glyn Jones. A year or more later, he wrote his story *The Orchards* [1]—'a hundred orchards on the road to the sea village'. Here the inverted name Llareggub first appears, in the phrase 'a story more terrible than the stories of the reverend madmen in the Black Book of Llareggub' (in *Under Milk Wood*, the lifework of the Reverend Eli Jenkins is the White Book of Llareggub). It is perhaps too fanciful to suggest a further link between Laugharne and *The Orchards*; but in a letter describing the Whitsun visit to Laugharne, 'the strangest town in Wales', he apostrophizes his pencil:

Let me, o oracle in the lead of the pencil, drop this customary clowning, and sprinkle some sweetheart words over the paper.

In *The Orchards*, as Vernon Watkins pointed out, the pencil is described in the act of making a poem:

He raised his pencil so that its shadow fell, a tower of wood and lead, on the clean paper; he fingered the pencil tower, the half-moon of his thumb-nail rising and setting behind the leaden spire. The tower fell, down fell the city of words, the walls of a poem, the symmetrical letters.

---

[1] First printed in *The Criterion*, vol. 15, no. 61, July 1936: later in *The Map of Love*, 1939.

The topography of the town of Llareggub, however, is based not so much on Laugharne, which lies on the mouth of an estuary, but rather on New Quay, a seaside town in Cardiganshire, with a steep main street running down to the harbour. Here, failing to get a house in Laugharne, Dylan rented a bungalow—'this wood-and-asbestos pagoda'—from 1944 to 1945; and New Quay is certainly 'the sea town' of the broadcast talk, *Quite Early One Morning*,[1] which was broadcast in the Welsh Home Service on 14th December 1944.

As is well known, *Quite Early One Morning* clearly foreshadows *Under Milk Wood*, both in theme and in phrasing:

The town was not yet awake . . . What big seas of dreams run in the captain's sleep? Over what blue-whaled waves did he sail . . . Tasselled table-cloths, ferns in pots, fading photographs of the bearded and censorious dead . . . the done-by-hand water-colours . . .

Mrs Ogmore Pritchard in person issues her commands:

Dust the china, feed the canary, sweep the drawing-room floor;
And before you let the sun in, mind he wipes his shoes.

In his preface to *Under Milk Wood* Dr Daniel Jones recalls that it was because of the success of *Quite Early One Morning* that Dylan contemplated 'a more extended work against the same kind of background'. According to his biographer, Constantine FitzGibbon, Dylan had already outlined the plot to Richard Hughes 'in 1943 or thereabouts', and to FitzGibbon himself, one afternoon in a Chelsea drinking club, 'a year or so later'. In the outline to Richard Hughes, the villagers, loving and giving,

---

[1] Printed in *Quite Early One Morning*, a collection of broadcasts by Dylan Thomas: 1954.

4

are interrogated by an inspector from London. After they have given their evidence, he regards them as condemned out of their own mouths, and certifies the whole village as insane. In the outline to FitzGibbon, the plot is extended; after the inspector's decision, the village is insulated by barbed wire and sentries, 'lest its dotty inhabitants infect the rest of the world with their feckless and futile view of life'.[1]

Dr Jones refers to the discussions between Dylan and his friends (after *Quite Early One Morning*) as to whether the work should be a stage play, a comedy in verse, or a radio play with a blind man as both narrator and central character. The title was to be *The Town was Mad*. In the outline given by Dr Jones, after the town is declared an insane area, blind Captain Cat insists on a formal trial in the town hall, with himself as Counsel for the Defence. But after hearing Counsel for the Prosecution describe the ideally sane town, the inhabitants 'withdraw their defence and beg to be cordoned off from the sane world as soon as possible'.

Mrs Vernon Watkins has written: [2]

I know that the idea of *Under Milk Wood*—the germ, rather, of the earliest idea, which as you know was totally different—was conceived while Dylan was at New Quay: but I remember him telling Vernon, at a cricket match in Swansea in, I'm almost sure, the early fifties, about it, and quoting a great deal, so that it must have been written by then. It was still, even then, in the form of a trial (you remember the village was to appear at a sort of tribunal to defend its sanity, or morality, or something): and the scene Dylan quoted was one in which one of the inhabi-

---

[1] Constantine FitzGibbon, *The Life of Dylan Thomas*, 1965: p. 269.
[2] Letters to Douglas Cleverdon, 9th and 18th February 1968,

tants [Jack Black] was confessing to increasingly more awful lusts or perversions (awful to the Welsh puritanism but of course really quite mild) and each confession was greeted by the jury with a horrified and delighted 'Ach-y-fi!'. . . .

I'm almost sure that he conceived it as a radio play, because he said, with one of his mischievous looks, that he wanted a really thunderous chorus of 'Ach-y-fi,'—'But I don't suppose the B.B.C. would feel like paying 150 male voices just to shout "Ach-y-fi".'

It seems most probable, then, that the idea germinated about the end of 1944, though it is unlikely that Dylan then started writing. But in June 1947 Philip Burton, then a B.B.C. producer in Wales, produced Dylan's radio feature on Swansea, *Return Journey*. As this was a very successful broadcast, Burton encouraged Dylan to undertake a work on a larger scale; and he recalls [1] a memorable session at the Café Royal in 1947, when Dylan outlined to him a work for radio with the tentative title, *The Village of the Mad*.

Meanwhile, from the autumn of 1945 to the end of 1948, much of Dylan's time was occupied in broadcasting. The film work was dropping off, and the American tours had not yet started; his main though intermittent source of income was the B.B.C. Aneirin Talfan Davies in Cardiff was mainly responsible for the broadcasting of Dylan's Welsh stories and reminiscences. Eric Blair ('George Orwell'), then a producer for the Eastern Service, had used him in 1943 as a poetry-reader. A couple of years later, when John Arlott produced a weekly series for the Eastern Service entitled *Book of*

---

[1] *Adam International Review:* Dylan Thomas Memorial Number, No. 238, 1953: p. 36. Reprinted in *Dylan Thomas: the Legend and the Poet*, ed. E. W. Tedlock, 1960.

Verse, Dylan took part in thirty or more programmes between September 1945 and December 1946. Patric Dickinson employed him in poetry programmes for the B.B.C. Home Service. So, on the B.B.C. Third Programme, did Roy Campbell (who once casually remarked, as a fact self-evident to poets, that the one advantage of being in the B.B.C. was that you could give jobs to your friends).

In the context of *Under Milk Wood*, however, it is worth considering in some detail Dylan's work as a radio actor rather than as a verse-reader.

Under the generous leadership of Laurence Gilliam, the B.B.C. Features Department was for twenty years the avant-garde of radio, and produced most of the outstanding programmes that were chosen as B.B.C. entries for the international Italia Prize (awarded to *Under Milk Wood*[1] in 1954). It was mainly for Features producers that Dylan worked as a radio actor. This not only afforded a companionable circle of like-minded radio practitioners; it also gave him an insight into the techniques of radio writing, which he himself was to develop still further.

Radio is *par excellence* the medium for the poet—not merely in its simplest form of enabling him to read his own poems aloud to his listeners. There is in radio no limit to the evocative power of words; it is the medium of

---

[1] For the Italia Prize, the B.B.C. submitted a sixty-minute recording, abridged from the ninety-five-minute production of 25th January 1954. Sixty copies of the script of this abridged version, with a French translation by Jacques Brunius, were issued by the B.B.C. for the use of the Italia Prize jury, and for other broadcasting organizations. By the end of 1955 *Under Milk Wood* had been translated and broadcast in over a dozen languages, including Polish and Japanese. The earliest translation, into German by Eric Fried, was broadcast in the B.B.C. German Service on 10th March 1954.

the ear alone. There are no film sets, no stage scenery, no television visuals, no spectacle of a public platform with table and jug of water, to hamper the creative imagination of the writer or to inhibit the response of his audience. A scene can last five seconds or thirty minutes; a skilfully phrased line of dialogue or narration can switch the scene instantaneously from 1066 to the 1960s, from a slum kitchen to a mountain top, or beyond the horizons of time and space. There may be the ancillary power of music; but the beginning and end of radio, as an art, is the spoken word.

Naturally, only a comparatively small proportion of the works produced by the B.B.C. Features Department aimed at the highest standards of poetic achievement. Many of them were actualities, or topical documentaries, or critical features like the series of *New Judgments*— Dylan took part in the *New Judgment on Edgar Allan Poe*. But if any producer wished to attempt some major work, Laurence Gilliam would give him every encouragement to do so. In this atmosphere, and in the denser air of the adjacent pubs, the *George* and the *Stag*, the art of radio was nourished. Of the twenty or so producers in Features Department, several were (or in their youth had been) poets themselves—Terence Tiller, Rayner Heppenstall, Louis MacNeice, Edward Sackville-West, D. G. Bridson, W. R. Rodgers; some of them were close friends of Dylan. So, considering his impoverishment, it was not only right and proper, but also natural that they should give him whatever jobs they could; for he was a natural actor, and, in his way, unique.

As a boy he had acted with the Swansea Grammar School Dramatic Society (taking the part of Cromwell in John Drinkwater's *Oliver Cromwell* in 1930); and had also played small parts with the Y.M.C.A. Players. Later, when he was on the staff of the *South Wales Daily Post*, from 1931 to 1934, he occasionally acted as an extra for the professional repertory company at the Grand Theatre, but found much wider scope with an amateur

8

dramatic group at the Swansea Little Theatre. Here he played a number of leading parts, from Witwoud in *The Way of the World* to Simon Bliss in *Hay Fever*. His first job as a radio actor was for a feature programme, *Sailors' Home*, produced by Francis Dillon in September 1941 for the B.B.C. Overseas Service. Then, in November 1942, he was engaged for my production of David Jones's magnificent epic of the First World War, *In Parenthesis*. This was scheduled for 10th November, the eve of Armistice Day. At the last moment the transmission was cancelled, to provide space for Churchill's speech from the Mansion House ('blood, toil, tears and sweat'). Later in the same month Dylan took part in *The British Tommy*, also produced by Francis Dillon; but he did not act on radio again until R. D. Smith engaged him for five productions in May and June, 1946, and commissioned him to write a script, *The Londoner*, in a series, *This is London*.

Dylan had been commissioned to write a couple of feature scripts for the Latin-American Service in 1940; but *The Londoner* is particularly interesting in that it is contained within the same framework as *Under Milk Wood*. It begins with narration:

> It's nearly half past six on a summer morning. Montrose Street is awake . . . But most of the houses are still sleeping. In Number 49, all is quiet. Lily Jackson is dreaming . . .

We hear the dreams of Lily Jackson and her husband Ted. After breakfast, Ted goes off to work, the children to school; Lily does the washing up and goes shopping. There is no great merit in the script, but it shows originality in Lily's verse-soliloquy as she does the household chores; and the women in the queue anticipate the gossiping neighbours in Mrs Organ Morgan's shop:

3RD SHOPPER: Pity the men can't queue a bit . . .
IST SHOPPER: How long you been queueing, dear?

9

3RD SHOPPER: I've been here half an hour.

2ND SHOPPER: I been queueing for six and a half years.

The programme ends with narration:

> It's a summer night now in Montrose Street. And
> the street is sleeping. In Number 49 all is quiet. The
> Jacksons are dreaming.

It was in October, 1946, that he first acted for Louis
MacNeice:

> And an extremely good actor he was. He took a great
> deal of trouble over it, and he also showed a great
> deal of enthusiasm, and I always tried to give him
> parts that he would enjoy—some of them grotesque,
> such as when he played a raven for me in a fairy
> story, and some of them quite serious, as when he
> played the historic part of Aristophanes.[1]

He played the Raven when (with Richard Burton as
Childe Roland) he took part in the 1950 production of
The Dark Tower, and he also played—again with Richard
Burton—in my 1946 and 1948 productions of David
Jones's *In Parenthesis*, a work for which both of them had
the profoundest admiration. In Washington, Dylan once
devoted an entire poetry reading to David Jones and John
Donne. In the broadcast of *In Parenthesis* he gave an
unforgettable performance as Private Dai Evans, and his
speaking of the Boast of Dai was superb. Richard Burton
has described the spine-chilling impact of Dai's 'Mam,
mam, don't let it!' as the shell screams down and bursts,
while on the right of the advancing line the Royal Welch,
'the genuine Taffies', sing to the tune of *Aberystwyth*:

> Dylan as an actor and as an explosive performing
> force was a dangerous rival for other actors, as I
> know, for I worked with him a few times or several,
> and once for instance a director said to him, we were

---

[1] Louis MacNeice in *Tribute to Dylan Thomas*, B.B.C.
Home Service, 9th December 1953.

rehearsing a radio play at the time, Dylan will you take the words 'Mam! Mam!' and scream them for me; you understand that you are dying in No Man's Land, and when you hear the Royal Welch sing, I will give you a cue light and then scream for me woodjew there's a good chap. And the Royal Welch did sing in the rehearsal, it was a record of course, and they sang of what you could see from the hills above Jerusalem, and was in the minor key and sad as the devil or death, and the green light flickered, and Dylan, short, bandy, prime, obese, and famous among the bars, screamed as I have never heard, but sometimes imagined a scream, and we were all appalled, our pencils silent above the crossword puzzles, and invisible centuries-gone atavistic hair rose on our backs. And there was a funny silence and Dylan said that he'd bet I couldn't do that scream like that with a cigarette in my mouth and I shook off the centuries, stopped staring, smiled a little, noted that he had indeed monumentally screamed with a cigarette in his mouth and went stunned back to my crossword.[1]

Among other parts that Dylan played for me, the longest and loudest was Satan in a complete *Paradise Lost*; of the poetry programmes, the most impressive was broadcast on 25th September 1950, when he read for me *Over Sir John's Hill*, *In Country Sleep* and *In the White Giant's Thigh*, with an introduction [2] describing a long

---

[1] From a review by Richard Burton of *The Life of Dylan Thomas* in *Book Week*, 24th October 1965. I am indebted to Professor Ralph Maud for bringing this review to my notice.

[2] Printed in *Quite Early One Morning*, 1954, pp. 155 ff. The following corrections may be noted: page 155, line 24, *for* danger *read* peril: p. 156, 1. 19, *for* bowler-out *read* bawler-out: p. 157, 1. 6, *for* call to *read* tell: 1. 11, *for* self-called *read* self-killed.

11

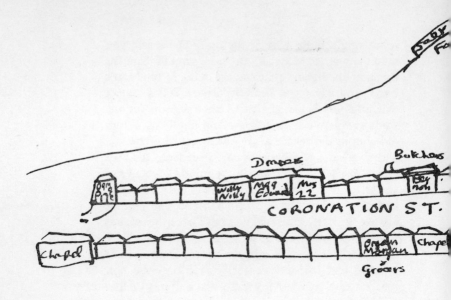

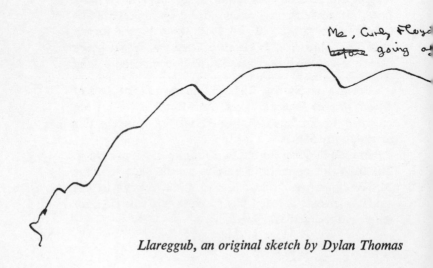

Llareggub, an original sketch by Dylan Thomas

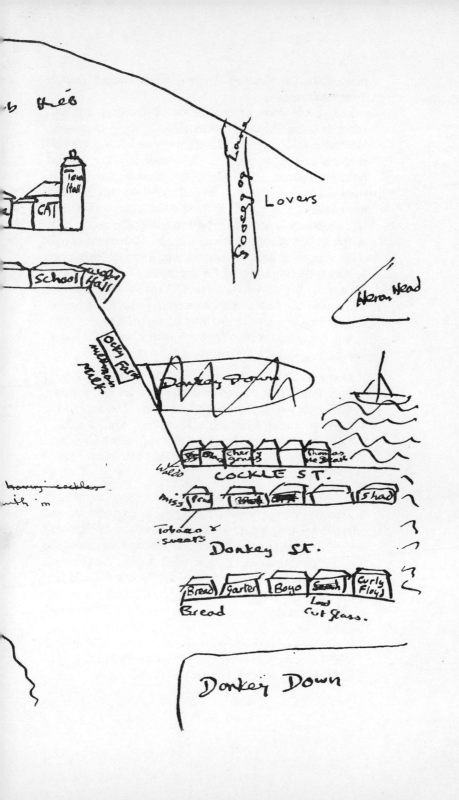

b fleb

Town Hall

CAT

Lovers Lane

Lovers

Heron Head

School Welfare Hall

Ocky Farm milkman milk

Donkey Down

Waldo COCKLE ST.

cher groes

Thomas the Death

having cockles with 'm

miss Price Polly Corn Shad

Tobacco & sweats Donkey St.

Bread garter Boyo Sarah Curly Floyd

Bread Lou cut Glass.

Donkey Down

poem-to-be, *In Country Heaven*, which would include these three poems.

I think it is worth putting on record that during B.B.C. rehearsals his standards were thoroughly professional. He had a wonderful ear for rhythms and inflexions and accents, and could apprehend immediately the subtlest points of interpretation. He was, moreover, sober, hard-working, and punctilious. So conscientious was he that I have known him leave a pub at lunch-time earlier than was necessary in order to return to the studio and con his script before the afternoon rehearsal. When rehearsals were over, of course, he relaxed; and I believe that when he was collecting material for documentary programmes, his normal habits were indulged. There was, for instance, a hilarious trip to Margate in company with R. D. Smith, then a Features producer, and Elizabeth Lutyens, who was to compose the music for the programme. The sequel has been recorded by Edith Sitwell:

> One day he came to lunch with me—that was the only time when I have seen him a little, perhaps a little over—d' you see? And he said, 'I'm sorry to smell so awful, Edith, it's Margate.' 'Oh,' I said, 'Yes, of course, my dear boy, naturally it's Margate. Of course, I quite understand that.' He'd just been to Margate.[1]

I had naturally assumed that the smell was of drink; but I recently learnt from R. D. Smith that during the Margate visit, on a cold winter day, the three of them had been walking along the dreary and deserted asphalt of the Dreamland Amusement Park, when Dylan caught sight of an automatic scent-spraying machine. He insisted that all three should be sprayed; and his own clothes were still reeking of scent when he came to lunch with Edith Sitwell.

---

[1] Edith Sitwell in *Portrait of Dylan Thomas*, B.B.C. Third Programme, 9th November 1963.

It was R. D. Smith who later suggested that Dylan should be invited to write a feature on Swansea in the series *Return Journey*. Features Department had devised this series in order to lure writers of distinction into the radio field; they were commissioned to return to their native town, or to some other place that had powerful associations for them, and to write a programme about it, in the form of a semi-autobiographical talk interspersed by dramatized flashbacks, extracts from journals, actuality recordings—anything, in fact, that might illuminate the theme. This proved an effective formula; among the couple of dozen writers who succumbed to the temptation were Sean O'Faolain, Eric Linklater, V. S. Pritchett, Christopher Sykes, Henry Reed and W. R. Rodgers. Dylan welcomed the proposal, and in February 1947 he and Reggie Smith spent three days in Swansea revisiting pubs and other places that Dylan had known before the blitz. The result was a script [1] that is a model of its kind, written with a wry nostalgic humour and with evocative overtones that reverberate in the mind like the park-keeper's bell in Cwmdonkin Park. With his poet's insight and his practical experience of broadcasting techniques, Dylan knew exactly how to create a work of permanent value from the fluid medium of radio. I doubt whether there has ever been a better thirty-minute radio piece. As it was concerned with a Welsh subject, the programme was produced in Cardiff by P. H. Burton, with Dylan as narrator and as himself. It was altogether an admirable production, and had an enthusiastic response from listeners and critics.

Return Journey brings us back to the project of the work for radio, *The Village of the Mad*, which Dylan outlined to Philip Burton in 1947. In a letter to his parents from Italy on 19th July, after describing the congratu-

---

[1] *Return Journey*, printed in *Quite Early One Morning*, 1954.

latory letters and press notices he has received for *Return Journey*, Dylan writes:

> I want very much to write a full-length—hour to hour & a half—broadcast play; and hope to do it, in South Leigh, this autumn.

No doubt this reflected the interest that Philip Burton had expressed, on behalf of the B.B.C., in *The Village of the Mad*. It is unlikely that Dylan wrote much of it at South Leigh, where he went to live on returning from Italy in August 1947. During the next fifteen months he took part in over forty broadcasts (each involving a visit to London), and was also script-writing for Gainsborough Films. When, in March 1949, he was invited by Elwyn Evans, a B.B.C. Talks Producer in Cardiff, to review a new edition of Gerard Manley Hopkins, he replied:

> I wish I could. But I've just got a new film-script to write and a play adaptation[1] for Third, and I mustn't take on any other job, even a 15 minute one . . .

There is no record elsewhere of any 'play adaptation for Third'; but this may have been a circuitous reference to *The Village of the Mad*. But in any case, distracted by the frequent journeys to London, with their attendant hangovers, and harassed by incessant money troubles (now alarmingly magnified by income tax demands), he was in no state to concentrate on creating a large-scale work for radio. What he really wanted was to get back to Wales. At last, in May 1949, he moved back to Laugharne, which must itself have been far more conducive to the writing of *Under Milk Wood* than a farmhouse in the Oxfordshire countryside. Here, it seems, in his little hut near the Boat House, he was able to settle down and write most of the first half of the script.[2]

---

[1] Probably *Peer Gynt*.

[2] Towards the end of 1949 there was a possibility that Dylan might join Features Department as a script-writer—writing 'imaginative scripts—*of my own*'. Louis

I have always been rather puzzled by the matter of *The Village of the Mad*. There is no doubt that he worked hard on it; yet the plot seems to me rather artificially contrived, and oddly uncharacteristic of Dylan's particular kind of creative genius. It may be that, once the basic idea had sprung from his fertile imagination, it was too carefully nourished. In matters where he was not expert, Dylan showed genuine humility; and I cannot help feeling that 'much discussion with friends' (in Dr Jones's phrase) may have led to the helpful but excessive elaboration of the original *donnée*.

Dylan may also have assumed that for a sixty- or ninety-minute script the B.B.C. would require him to furnish a proper dramatic plot. Nobody outside the B.B.C. (and, indeed, comparatively few inside) can be expected to distinguish between a radio play and a radio feature. A radio play is a dramatic work deriving from the tradition of the theatre, but conceived in terms of radio. A radio feature is, roughly, any constructed programme (that is, other than news bulletins, racing commentaries, and so forth) that derives from the technical apparatus of radio (microphone, control-panel, recording gear, loud-speaker). It can combine any sound elements— words, music, sound effects—in any form or mixture of forms—documentary, actuality, dramatized, poetic, musico-dramatic. It has no rules determining what can or cannot be done. And though it may be in dramatic form, it has no need of a dramatic plot. Consequently, when the development of *The Village of the Mad* proved complicated, it was natural that Dylan should turn to the more fluid form of the feature. He did not totally discard the plot until 1950 or early 1951.

MacNeice was going to Athens for a couple of years, and Laurence Gilliam had the notion of inviting Dylan to take his post temporarily. Unfortunately the plan fell through, and Dylan remained a free-lance script-writer in Laugharne.

Meanwhile Philip Burton had been appointed Chief Instructor to the B.B.C. Staff Training School in London, and was no longer a producer. From the time when I first heard of Dylan's projected work for radio, I had been keenly interested in it; so lest the project should fall by the wayside, Philip Burton bequeathed it to me (though I was myself a Features Producer in London, I was at any rate Welsh on my mother's side).

At what stage Dylan drifted from the dramatic form of *The Village of the Mad* to the feature form of *Under Milk Wood* is uncertain. It seems to me probable that when he began to write the long, opening sequence of the dreamers in 'the lulled and dumbfound town', the feature form imposed itself upon him, and he continued in the same vein. The sleepers are rung out of sleep by the town hall bell, and (except for Mrs Pugh) come downstairs to breakfast. The shops squeak open, the children are shrilled off to school, and Captain Cat listens to the women gossiping round the pump. By now, a third of the final script was written, without establishing the vestige of a plot, or even providing a possible lead-in to the trial scenes that he had already written.

Towards the end of 1950, knowing that he was particularly penniless, Laurence Gilliam and I took Dylan out and asked him what he would like to do for quick and easy money. Interestingly, he suggested a programme on Edgar Lee Masters's *Spoon River Anthology*, the sequence of poems in which the dead of a town in the Middle West speak, from the graveyard, their honest epitaphs; possibly anticipating Rosie Probert speaking from the bedroom of her dust. He and I met again on 11th December to discuss the choice of poems for the programme, which had to be done quickly if the money was to be paid quickly.[1]

---

[1] In spite of telegrams, the script of his commentary failed to arrive. As all routine bookings had been completed, my final (reply-paid) telegram warned him that

18

It was at this meeting that we also discussed the *Madtown* (as he then called it). But I cannot remember whether it was then or on some later occasion that I suggested the obvious solution—that he should drop the plot altogether, and simply carry on with the life of the town until nightfall. He seemed relieved at this proposal, and accepted it without demur (though John Davenport wrote later of his disappointment at failing to fulfil his original scheme).[1]

It was not long after this, I think, that he and his wife Caitlin came to dinner, and he read the script aloud to us. How far it had progressed at this stage, I cannot now recall; but as at that time I had not read any part of it, its effect was overwhelming. The writing, however, progressed slowly. From time to time he assured me that there was nothing he wanted more than to complete *Under Milk Wood*; but he was obliged to spend his time on small jobs that brought immediate cash returns. I sympathized with him in this dilemma, and was able to persuade the B.B.C. to take the unprecedented step of offering, on account, five guineas for every thousand words; but this made little difference. On another occasion Laurence Gilliam suggested that I should visit Laugharne myself in order to urge him on. This was equally fruitless, though it proved an enjoyable and eventful weekend. One accepted the producer's occupational risk of maintaining the honour of the B.B.C. by drinking pint for pint with Dylan on an empty stomach until half an hour or so after closing time; but then, instead of returning to the Boat House and supper, we

---

we were facing disaster; his reply bade me 'Unface disaster script and self coming.' But neither script nor self appeared. The script was finally written in August 1952: and then only by making arrangements for him to be locked in the B.B.C. Reference Library all night.

[1] *Dylan Thomas: the Legend and the Poet*, ed. E. W. Tedlock, 1960: p. 80.

went in again through the back door of the pub and stayed for another couple of hours.

It is very easy, of course—especially if one has a monthly paid income—to recall such occasions as this with tolerant amusement. But one need only read Dylan's letters during these later years to realize his tragic situation—'this nervous hag that rides me, biting and scratching into insomnia, nightmare, and the long anxious daylight'.

The successive letters to Countess Caetani show the desperate shifts to which he was reduced. Two of the letters concern *Under Milk Wood*. In October 1951 he sent her the unfinished script, under the title *Llareggub. A Piece for Radio Perhaps*. In the long accompanying letter, he describes it as:

the first half of something I am delighting in doing and which I shall complete very shortly. Only very special circumstances are preventing me from carrying on with it every minute of the working day.

He then refers to a play, mostly in verse, which he has reluctantly but only temporarily abandoned; 'the comedy was lost in the complicated violence of the words'. This is presumably *The Village of the Mad*; but out of his working on it, he says, came the idea of *Llareggub*:

(Please ignore it as a final title.) Out of it came the idea that I write a piece, a play, an impression for voices, an entertainment out of the darkness of the town I live in, and to write it simply and warmly & comically with lots of movement and varieties of moods, so that, at many levels, through sight and speech, description & dialogue, evocation and parody, you come to know the town as an inhabitant of it.[1]

---

[1] *Botteghe Oscure*, Quaderno XIII, Rome 1954: p. 94. Reprinted in *Selected Letters of Dylan Thomas*, ed. Constantine FitzGibbon, 1966: pp. 363–6.

He describes how the piece will develop, through the long lazy lyrical afternoon, into the night, and silence. Two voices will be predominant—the preacher, 'who talks only in verse', and the anonymous chronicler called IST VOICE. Then, after a brilliant verbal cadenza describing the various characters, he comes to the heart of the matter. Could she send him, and at once, £100 in payment for the whole script? He can finish it in two weeks. They have to leave Laugharne—the house is sold; but they cannot leave without paying the whole of the debts he owes in the town, amounting to about £100.

Twelve months later, on 6th November 1952, he sends her one of his masterpieces of apology (on which, as FitzGibbon records, he would spend days, or even weeks), and promises the rest of *Under Milk Wood* for 1st February. Meanwhile, in May 1952, Countess Caetani had published the incomplete script in her quarterly, *Botteghe Oscure*, using the provisional title of *Llareggub, a Piece for Radio Perhaps*.

BOTTEGHE OSCURE

The *Botteghe Oscure* version (referred to as BO) ranks, then, as the first printing of *Under Milk Wood*. It ends on page 43, line 6, of the first English edition (published by J. M. Dent & Sons Ltd in 1954: referred to as D) and on page 48, line 3, of the first American edition (published by New Directions in 1954: referred to as ND) with Captain Cat's line:

Organ Morgan's at it early. You can tell it's Spring.

(D 43, 6: ND 48, 3) [1]

BO does not contain the following:

The passage on Evans the Death.

(D 8, 4–15: ND 9, 1–12)

1ST VOICE: In Butcher Beynon's, Gossamer Beynon, [*to*]
GOSSAMER BEYNON: My foxy darling.

(D 16, 9–20, 6: ND 18, 6–22, 15)

2ND VOICE: He intricately rhymes [*to*]
her frock that brushes the dew.

(D 20, 28–22, 4: ND 23, 11–24, 23)

The scene of Mr and Mrs Cherry Owen.

(D 32, 20–34, 17: ND 36, 12–38, 19)

Willy Nilly Postman on his rounds.

(D 38, 22–42, 2: ND 43, 8–46, 23)

Other passages where BO differs from D are:

An extra verse in the Reverend Eli Jenkins's morning poem. (D 25: ND 28)

---

[1] Page numerals are printed throughout in 'modern' figures (0123456789): line numbers in 'old style' (0123456789).

Polly Garter's soliloquy (D 30: ND 34) is shorter, and ends:

and listening to the voices of the blooming birds who seem to say to me

CHILDREN'S VOICES (*singsonging, one after the other on different notes*): Polly
Love [etc. See p. 76]

Love [etc. See p. 76]

Captain Cat's soliloquy on the women (D 42: ND 47) is shorter, and ends with his joining in with children singing 'One, two, buckle my shoe'.

STAGE II

NEW YORK, MAY 1953

Between October 1951, when Dylan sent the unfinished
script to Countess Caetani, and 14th May 1953, when the
first stage-reading with a cast was given in New York, he
enlarged the *Botteghe Oscure* version, and wrote most of
the remainder of the script. He left for his third American
tour on 16th April 1953, taking a script of *Under Milk
Wood* with him. On 3rd May he read the whole of it
himself at the Fogg Museum, Harvard. Then, on 14th
May, he gave the first of two stage readings at the Poetry
Center of the Young Men's and Young Women's Hebrew
Association in New York.

It is said that before the solo reading at Harvard on
3rd May, and before each of the two stage-readings in
New York on 14th and 28th May, Dylan was writing
additional material up to the very last moment. Elizabeth
Reitell, who was then the secretary of the Poetry Center,
has recorded her recollection of 14th May:

The curtain was going to rise at 8.40. Well, at 8.10
Dylan was locked in the backroom with me. And no
end to *Under Milk Wood*. He kept saying 'I can't, I
simply can't do this.' I said 'You can, the curtain is
going to go up.' Strangely enough he wrote the very
end of *Under Milk Wood* then and there, and he
wrote the lead-up to it. He would scribble it down, I
would copy it, print it so that the secretary could
read it, hand it to John Brinnin, and hand it to the
secretary, do six copies. We all jumped into a cab
finally, and got over to the theatre at half-past eight
and handed out the six copies to the actors.[1]

[1] Elizabeth Reitell in *Portrait of Dylan Thomas*: B.B.C.
Third Programme, 9th November 1963.

Fortunately the stage-reading on 14th May was recorded, and was subsequently issued commercially by Caedmon Publishers in New York. As the recording, in a large hall with an audience, was arranged almost at the last moment on an ordinary tape-recorder, it is not technically perfect; but it is, of course, of the greatest interest in that Dylan himself took the parts of 1ST VOICE and the REVEREND ELI JENKINS (and the small parts of SECOND and FIFTH DROWNED), and directed the other five readers. Moreover, as no complete script of the stage-reading of 14th May is known to exist, the Caedmon recording is the authentic text-source.

The main additions in the Caedmon recording (C) to the *Botteghe Oscure* version (BO) were:

1ST VOICE: In Butcher Beynon's, Gossamer Beynon, [*to*] He drinks the fish.
(D 16, 19–18, 4: ND 18, 7–20, 4)

2ND VOICE: Willy Nilly, postman, [*to*]
GOSSAMER BENYON: My foxy darling.
(D 18, 15–20, 6: ND 20, 16–22, 15)

The scene of Mr and Mrs Cherry Owen, except the last five speeches. (D 32, 20–34, 2: ND 36, 12–38, 4) Willy Nilly on his rounds (D 38–42: ND 43–46), including the two passages (subsequently cut) on the lodger at Craig-y-don (see footnote on p. 86). Several passages in the sequence were later rewritten.

C also contains the following passages from BO, rewritten in their final form:

The passage on Mae Rose Cottage.
(D 19, 4–13: ND 21, 8–17)
The passage on Willy Nilly and Mrs Willy Nilly.
(D 31, 27–32, 6: ND 35, 11–22)
Captain Cat's soliloquy on the women (D 42: ND 47). The children's song 'Polly, Love' (see p. 76) was cut.

The remainder of the C text (i.e. completing the

unfinished BO version) is identical with D and ND, except that it does not include:

1ST VOICE: Captain Cat, at his window [*to*]
      as he sleeps and sails.

(D 68, 10–19: ND 75, 9–18) [1]

Now the town is dusk (including the Ogmore Pritchard scene) [*to*]
And then you must take them off.

(D 76, 23–78, 9: ND 84, 12–86, 8)

1ST VOICE: And at the doorway of Bethesda House (including the Reverend Eli Jenkins's Sunset Poem) [*to*]
And say, good-bye—but just for now!

(D 78, 24–79, 17: ND 86, 23–87, 17)

SINBAD: Evening, Cherry [*to*]
      on the tombstone on his way home.

(D 80, 16–85, 7: ND 88, 19–93, 20)

Part of the typescript that Dylan used for the stage-reading on 14th May has survived as approximately the second half of MS, the script that he delivered to the B.B.C. (see p. 31). It seems to have been typed in U.S.A., presumably at the Poetry Center, on paper of a texture that is common in U.S.A. but not in England. The spelling are frequently American ('thru' for 'through'), and some words have evidently baffled the New York typist (see footnote on 'Twll', p. 95).

This typescript has been heavily corrected in pencil and/or ink in many passages, and is of considerable interest as evidence of the development of the text during and after the New York readings. As a general rule it seems that (as one might expect) pencil was used during rehearsals to adapt the script for the stage-reading. These alterations were usually intended to take the place of sound effects, and to mark insertions of additional material, or to make references intelligible for an

---

[1] In C, this passage follows the text of the deleted typescript of MS (see pp. 108–9).

26

American audience (e.g. 'J.P.'s' expanded to 'Justices of the Peace'). The pencil insertions also include production notes in Dylan's hand, as he not only read 1ST VOICE and THE REVEREND ELI JENKINS, but also directed the stage-reading. As they have the validity of printed directions, they have been included in the Analysis of Variants.

Ink was normally used either to clarify or confirm a pencil alteration, to *stet* an original passage, or to mark insertions of additional material; the alterations in ink seem, for the most part, to have been made after Dylan's return from New York. In the Analysis of Variants, reference is made to ink or pencil when there seems some possible significance.

By comparing this typescript with the text of C, we can deduce with some confidence which passages were added for 14th May and 28th May respectively, and which were added after Dylan's departure from New York in June 1953. The typescript does not include the first half of MS (written by hand as a fair copy), but consists of:

MRS CHERRY OWEN: And then you did a little dance on
            the table [*to*]
for the second dark time this one spring day.
            (D 33, 24–86, 15: ND 37, 22–95, 8)

It lacks the following section (added during the New York readings in October 1953):

1ST VOICE: Dusk is drowned for ever [*to*]
a wife out of flowers.
            (D 81, 3–82, 27: ND 89, 9–91, 8)

The pagination of this extant typescript runs thus: 20–21, 21A, 22–48, 48a, 49, 50, 51.

Typescript pages 20–48 (to the line 'given it a lump of sugar': D 76, 22: ND 84, 14) were apparently complete before rehearsals started for the 14th May stage-reading, and are contained in the Caedmon recording (C). This main script probably contained also the Mae Rose Cottage sequence as far as 'she tells the goats': (D 78,

9–17: ND 86, 9–17); it was apparently cut from the bottom of 48 and inserted at the bottom of 48a.

The remainder is largely made up of typed slips of paper Sellotaped together, with some manuscript pages inserted. This remaining section can be divided into three groups:

(1) Passages typed on yellow flimsy paper for the stage-reading on 14th May, and therefore in Caedmon recording:

MAE ROSE COTTAGE: You just wait [to]
The goats champ and sneer.

(D 78, 18–22: ND 86, 18–22)

1ST VOICE: Jack Black prepares [to]
Off to Gomorrah!   (D 79, 18–25: ND 87, 18–25)

1ST VOICE: And Cherry Owen, sober as Sunday [to]
Because I love them both.

(D 80, 1–15: ND 88, 4–18)

Mr Mog Edwards and Miss Myfanwy Price [to]
this one Spring day.   (D 85, 8–86, 15: ND 93, 21–95, 8)

(2) Passages typed on white flimsy paper for the stage-reading on 28th May, and therefore *not* in Caedmon recording:

Now the town is dusk [to]
And then you must take them off.

(D 76, 23–78, 8: ND 84, 15–86, 8)

2ND VOICE: And Lily Smalls is up to Nogood Boyo in the washhouse.   (D 79, 26–28: ND 88, 1–3. Written in pencil on p. 49 of typescript)

SINBAD: Evening, Cherry [to]
. . . oh Gossamer, open yours!

(D 80, 16–81, 2: ND 88, 19–89, 8)

(3) Manuscript passages inserted after Dylan's return to England on 3rd June, and before his departure for New York on 19th October:

1ST VOICE: And at the doorway of Bethesda House, [to]

28

And say, good-bye—but just for now!

(D 78, 23–79, 17: ND 86, 23–87, 17)

2ND VOICE: Mr Waldo, in his corner [to]
Bring along your chimbley brush!

(D 82, 28–83, 31: ND 91, 9–92, 13)

These last two passages (the Reverend Eli Jenkins's Sunset Poem and Mr Waldo's Song) will be considered in more detail in the following section.

THE MANUSCRIPT

It appears that after his return from New York in June 1953 Dylan began to revise and copy out by hand the corrected typescript that he had used for the May recitals. This incomplete fair copy, neatly written in his schoolboyish hand, consists of twenty-three foolscap pages. (These pages have only minor corrections, except for page 17, which contains Lily Smalls's poem, 'Oh, there's a face!' (D 26: ND 29) with a couple of additional stanzas, deleted.) The fair copy ends with the last line of the Cherry Owen scene, 'you snored all night like a brewery' (D 34, 15–16: ND 38, 18). As these twenty-three manuscript pages replace the first nineteen pages of the typescript used for the New York stage-readings, one cannot be quite certain that all the additions noted here were added *after* Dylan returned to England. But it looks to me as though pages 1 to 11 of the manuscript comprised a final revised version, with only one additional passage (on Evans the Death: D 8, 4–15: ND 9, 1–12). Pages 12 to 23 consisted, as it were, of a semi-final revision, incorporating the following main additions and rewritings:

The passages on P.C. Atilla Rees and his helmet (D 18, 5–14, and 28, 21–23: ND 20, 5–14, and 28, 21–23)

The rewritten passage on Mae Rose Cottage (D 19, 3–12: ND 21, 8–17)

The lengthened passage (incorporating an additional passage on Mary Ann the Sailors) [*from*]

The Reverend Eli Jenkins, poet, preacher, [*to*]

her frock that brushes the dew.

(D 20, 22–22, 4: ND 23, 6–24, 23)

Two additional stanzas (both deleted) in Lily Smalls's poem (D 26: ND 29)

Lengthened speeches of Mrs Dai Bread One (D 29, 20–27: ND 33, 7–14), Mrs Dai Bread Two (D 30, 1–9: ND 33, 15–22) and Polly Garter (D 30, 23–31, 2: ND 34, 10–18)

The lengthened scene of Mr and Mrs Cherry Owen [*from*]

See that smudge on the wall [*to*]

snored all night like a brewery.   (D 32–34: ND 36–38)

This, unfortunately, was as far as Dylan got with his revision. The manuscript so far was a dream sequence, with few realistic effects. That he was still considering it, however, as a *Piece for Radio*, with or without *Perhaps*, is clear, I think, from the radio directions for Mae Rose Cottage (*Very close and softly*) (D 19: ND 21) and Mr Pugh at the top of the stair (*Door creaks open*) (D 27: ND 31).

The remainder of the text, however, in typescript, was in an extremely disordered state, for several reasons:

(1) The basic radio script had been typed by an American typist to whom some of the words were unintelligible.

(2) The typescript was then used for the rehearsals of the stage-reading on 14th May. Some words and phrases seem to have been altered or cut in rehearsal; and many of the sound effects (which in radio would have proved most evocative) were deleted or turned into narration. One example may suffice (it follows Captain Cat's comments on the children as they run off to school: D 38: ND 43). The typescript runs thus:

> (*The children's voices & noises fade
> Out school bell
> Clip-clop of Horse's feet on cobbles*)
> CAPTAIN CAT (*loudly*): Morning Big Ben.
> MAN'S VOICE: Morning, Captain.
> (*Clip-clop fades
> Noise of child running on cobbles*)

31

CAPTAIN CAT: (*softly*) Glyndur Jones, late again.
(*loudly*) You'll cop it, Glyndur [*sic for Glyndwr*]. Put a book down your breeches.

(*Noise of child on cobbles fades*)

Various emendations were made during rehearsal (MAN's VOICE was allocated to 'Al', presumably Allan F. Collins, one of the six readers). Finally, the whole sequence was reduced to the line that now appears in the printed text:

IST VOICE: And the children's voices cry away.

(D 38, 21: ND 43, 7)

(3) Dylan superimposed on the typescript his own production notes, with various markings which may or may not have textual significance.

(4) He made occasional alterations for the sake of his New York audience. For the second stage-reading on 28th May, for instance, Mr Beynon's 'corgies' (D 36, 5: ND 40, 16) were altered to 'squirrels' (and in the version printed later in *Mademoiselle*, to 'spaniels'). The reference to the envelope for the lodger in Craig-y-don was received in dead silence by the 14th May audience in the Caedmon recording; so it was deleted for the 28th May reading (see footnote on p. 86).

(5) He then restored some of the deletions (presumably after his return to England). The New York squirrels, for example, were turned back into Welsh corgies again. But the operation was not carried out with much care or consistency, for Dylan clearly intended to make a fair copy of the finally revised script.

(6) A further complication in the text arose from Dylan's giving a solo reading of *Under Milk Wood* to Tenby Arts Club in October 1953. For his Tenby audience, Dylan bracketed one speech, marked 'Not for Now', and deleted three other passages in faint pencil, marked 'Not for Tenby' or 'Out for Tenby'.

The bracketed speech was that of *Voice of a Guide Book* (D 23: ND 25–26). For a solo reader, this comic parody would have broken the poetic mood of the narration that precedes and follows it. No doubt Dylan could have carried it off successfully enough; but it seems to me a sensible cut. The pencilled 'Not for Now' was later deleted in ink.

The first deleted passage followed Sinbad's line, 'I dote on that Gossamer Beynon' (D 55, 18: ND 61, 21: for the text, see pp. 100–1 and footnote). The pencil note 'Out for Tenby' was later deleted in ink.

In the second deleted passage ('And if only grandma'd die [to] again.' D 55, 27–56, 12: ND 62, 8–22) the pencil note 'Out for Tenby' was later deleted in ink, with the word Stet.

These two passages were obviously deleted because a solo reader could not simultaneously speak the lines and sing the children's song.

The third deleted passage ('She feels his goatbeard tickle her . . .' D 61, 23–28: ND 68, 12–17) is deleted in pencil with the note 'Not for Tenby'. This note was later deleted in ink, with the word Stet.

It is very probable, of course, that Dylan would never have completed the script of *Under Milk Wood* if he had not been spurred on by the prospect of the New York readings, which offered immediate rewards and lucrative prospects. A few days after leaving New York, he wrote on 16th June 1953 to John Malcolm Brinnin (who had organized his previous tours, and was to arrange the stage-readings in October):

> I'm going to start work tomorrow, and shall revise Milk Wood for publication and broadcasting here. I'll also be seeing David Higham [Dylan's literary agent] soon, and will get Milk Wood copyrighted as a play for public performance.[1]

There was one complication, however, arising out of an

---

[1] *Selected Letters of Dylan Thomas,* ed. Constantine FitzGibbon, p. 406.

advance that Dylan had been given in 1952 by the publishing firm of Wingate Ltd for a book of American impressions. As he had failed to deliver this, Wingate's threatened in 1953 to sue him for the return of the advance. David Higham persuaded them to accept an option on *Under Milk Wood* instead; but after seeing the unfinished MS., they unwisely preferred to sell the option to Dent's for the amount of the advance.

On 11th September Dylan wrote to E. F. Bozman of Dent's:

. . . I go to the States early in October. Well before I leave, I'll have finished the final corrections and amplifications of *Under Milk Wood*. I think it's much better now—(it sounds as though it had been ill). One of the reasons I'm going to America is to take part in three public readings of it, with a professional cast, at the Poetry Center, New York. (The other, and main, reason is to go to California to begin work with Stravinsky on a new opera.) And, when I return some time in December, I hope that it can be given one or two more reading-performances, most likely on a Sunday night, in London; with any luck, I'll be able to get firstrate Welsh actors to read it. Higham, in the meantime, and as soon as he has my complete version, will see to it that someone like Sherek has a chance of reading it with this in mind. *Under Milk Wood* will also be broadcast next year, in full, and it should be possible to arrange this broadcast to happen about the same time as publication. I myself have good hopes altogether of the success of *Milk Wood*; and I'm *very very* grateful to you for taking it over.[1]

Meanwhile news had reached me at the B.B.C. that the script was finished. It sounded (and was) too good to be

---

[1] *Selected Letters of Dylan Thomas*, ed. Constantine FitzGibbon, p. 413.

true. However, it was arranged that Dylan, David Higham and I should meet at Simpson's in the Strand for dinner on Monday, 12th October, and that I should then receive the script. Dylan did not arrive—apparently he lacked the money for the train-fare from Carmarthen; but I was assured that he would bring the script to me at the B.B.C. on Thursday.

The events of the following weekend have already had ample publicity.[1] But as they affected the development of the text, a final recapitulation may be useful. Dylan arrived at the B.B.C. with the script at lunch time on Thursday, and explained that he must have it back by Saturday; it was his only copy, and he would need it for the stage-reading in New York; his flight had been booked for Monday evening, the 19th. My secretary, Elizabeth Fox, accordingly typed the script on duplicating stencils, and gave it back to him when he called at the B.B.C. on Saturday morning.

During the weekend he telephoned me at home, in some agitation, to say that he had lost the manuscript, either in a taxi or in a pub. I assured him that I could get the script duplicated on Monday, and would bring copies to him at the Victoria Air Terminal before he left for New York. I met him on the Monday evening, and, to his evident relief, gave him three copies. As we were having a farewell drink before the coach started for the airport, I said

---

[1] In the High Court of Justice: Chancery Division: before Mr Justice Plowman. Thomas *v.* The Times Book Company Limited. An action by Mrs Caitlin Thomas to recover from The Times Book Co. Ltd the manuscript of *Under Milk Wood*, March 8–11, 1966. The action failed, and costs were awarded against the plaintiff in favour of The Times Book Company and of the third and fourth parties, J. Stevens Cox and Douglas Cleverdon. A limited edition of one hundred copies of the *Judgment*, edited by J. Stevens Cox, was published by the Toucan Press, Guernsey, C.I., 1967.

how sorry I was that the manuscript had been lost; he replied that if I could find it I could keep it; and he gave me the names of three or four pubs in which he might have left it. A couple of days later I found it in the Helvetia in Old Compton Street, Soho.

As described already on pp. 30–3, it consisted of pages 1 to 23 in manuscript; overlapping pages 20 to 51 in typescript (with manuscript insertions and corrections); and manuscript pages containing the Reverend Eli Jenkins's Sunset Poem and Mr Waldo's Song of the Chimbley Sweep. The Poem and the Song were working drafts written on leaves torn from an exercise book, with an introductory line of narration for each, with deleted drafts of the last verse of the Sunset Poem, and with an additional eight-line stanza, deleted, of Mr Waldo's Song (for text, see p. 121).

I was, of course, delighted to have the script at last. But it was quite clearly not in its final form; and this was confirmed by a list written on the verso of the page containing Mr Waldo's Song. The list, presumably written before the Song or the Sunset Poem, ran thus:

More Stuff for Actors to say

Song by Mr Waldo
Poem by the Rev.
Song by Thomas the Death
Song by Lily Smalls
Conversation, over cockles, between Mr & Mrs Floyd the cocklers
Ocky Milkman talking to his non-existent wife
All the Dai Breads together, before the dance
Nightmare by Lord Cut-glass.
P.C. Atilla & poachers

[*Note: added later in different ink*] He is so suspicious that, when they tell him they are going right, he goes left. They *always* tell him the truth.

Pub stuff
Voices for gravestones, Epitaphs,[1] with comments
Sinbad Sailors fearing the dark
Mrs Willy Nilly telling fear-stories to Willy-Nilly and
children [*Note in margin of last two lines*] good

There are also a couple of entries on the second leaf of the
Sunset Poem:

Lily Smalls, who harmlessly believes that one day she
will marry a Shah.

There are cave-paintings, painted by Mrs Beynon's
Billy. He also runs a side line of flint arrows.

The speed with which my secretary had to type the 71-
page script by Saturday morning meant that there was no
time to revise or check the text before duplicating. There
were, however, few typing errors. The only significant one
was 'grassfield', a misreading of 'goosefield' in the line
'snow lies deep on the goosefield' (D 8, 9: ND 9, 6).
Possibly forgetting the original, Dylan altered 'grassfield' to 'greenfield' for the New York readings on 24th
and 25th October.

As the manuscript had now been recovered, I was able
to check the B.B.C. duplicated script (referred to as B1).
The only serious omission was the passage (following
D 55, 18: ND 61, 21: text on p. 100) which had originally
been deleted in pencil with the note 'Out for Tenby'. This
note had later been deleted in ink; but as the passage had
not been marked *Stet*, my secretary omitted it from the
stencilled script. Another omission was in a line (D 79, 15)
in the Reverend Eli Jenkins's Sunset Poem. In the first
MS. draft Dylan wrote

Bless us this holy night, I pray,

Without deleting 'holy', he wrote above it 'long dark';

---

[1] Perhaps derived from Edgar Lee Masters, *Spoon
River Anthology*. See p. 18.

37

deleting 'long dark', he wrote above it 'winding'. In the second MS. draft, he retained 'winding'. In the third and final MS. draft, he wrote 'winding' and then deleted it, but without replacing 'holy'. My secretary accordingly typed the line as:

Bless us this night, I pray,

The deletions in these two passages subsequently led to a comic but infuriating dispute during the B.B.C. rehearsals, and (as will be described later) to omissions in the printed texts (D and ND).

NEW YORK, OCTOBER 1953

Meanwhile Dylan, with his three copies of B1, had arrived in New York early on 20th October; and rehearsals began immediately for the stage-readings at the YM–YWHA Poetry Center on 24th and 25th October. He used one copy of B1 for the rehearsals, correcting a few errors in typing and punctuation, making occasional cuts and emendations (e.g. for an American audience, 'gypsies'' for 'gyppo's'), replacing some sound effects by narration, and adding some production notes. This corrected copy is referred to as N1.[1] He inserted (after 'I dote on that Gossamer Beynon': D 55, 18: ND 61, 21) the missing passage that had been deleted with the note 'Out for Tenby' (see p. 37), and inserted the word 'holy' so that the line finally read:

> Bless us this holy night, I pray,

In the evening sequence, he added an extra page of script, containing:

> 1ST VOICE: Dusk is drowned forever until tomorrow [*to*] Where the old wizards made themselves a wife out of flowers.   (D 81, 3–82, 27: ND 89, 9–91, 8)

His main cuts were:

> 3RD WOMAN: Seen Mrs Butcher Beynon? [*to*] he's trying to pull it off and eat it.
>   (D 45, 18–27: ND 50, 18–51, 4)

---

[1] I am greatly indebted to Miss Elizabeth Reitell for having given me in 1957 a photostat of this script with Dylan's corrections.

MRS OGMORE-PRITCHARD: Husbands, [*to*]
And then you must take them off.

(D 77, 16–78, 8: ND 85, 10–86, 8)

I should mention here that there exists a duplicated
script, quarto, apparently prepared by Kenn Mileston.
In this script, Kenn Mileston has transcribed a few notes
by Dylan that are not recorded elsewhere. He gave me a
copy of the script in 1957; but I have lost touch with him
since, and have not been able to discover in what circumstances this script was used. In the Analysis of Variants I
have recorded any significant notes under the reference
N3.

Concerning the above cut relating to Mrs Ogmore-
Pritchard and her husband's pyjamas, Kenn Mileston has
a note:

I'm sure you see the terrible inference here, and why
he [Dylan] cut it out.

I have searched the recesses of my subconscious mind for
some esoteric obscenity in these lines, but can find only
the obvious one: which seems to me much less startling
than, for example, the description, a few lines earlier, of
Mrs Ogmore-Pritchard sitting 'erect as a dry dream'.
But perhaps nobody noticed that one.

The two stage-readings of *Under Milk Wood* took place
at the Kaufmann Auditorium, New York, on Saturday
evening and Sunday afternoon, 24th and 25th October,
under the sponsorship of the YM–YWHA Poetry Center.
The strain of the rehearsals seems to have been too great;
Dylan was already in a state of near collapse with a
mixture of cortisone drugs, alcohol and sleeping pills; but
during the next few days he managed to send the final
revisions of *Under Milk Wood*, with some cuts, to the
editor of *Mademoiselle* for an abridged version that was
published in February 1954. On 5th November he was
taken to hospital, and died on 9th November 1953.

THE B.B.C. PRODUCTION

Had Dylan lived, of course, he would have taken the part of the *First Voice* in the broadcast production. It happened that in January 1954 Richard Burton was acting at the Old Vic; although he was then playing Hamlet and rehearsing for Coriolanus, he undertook to play Dylan's part in *Under Milk Wood*. As for the music, Dylan and I had previously agreed that the songs of Polly Garter and the children should be set by the Welsh composer, Dr Daniel Jones, his lifelong friend in Swansea. I accordingly sent a script of B1 to Dr Jones (who had now become literary trustee for the Dylan Thomas Estate) and arranged with him to record the children's songs in Laugharne School.

Meanwhile, in New York, Elizabeth Reitell and Ruthven Todd had used a copy of B1 to compile a corrected script (referred to as N2) based on Dylan's N1. It bears a pencil note on title:

> Copy as finally corrected with inserts and cuts from the author's last working script. Copied for New Directions by Ruthven Todd and Liz Reitell from a copy in the possession of Miss Reitell. Brought to R. MacGregor, New Directions, by Ruthven Todd, Nov. 1953. A note in the book should explain that Dylan intended to work over the play again before it was printed. This version was the last prepared by him.

N2 is occasionally useful in clarifying an unclear correction of Dylan's in N1. But it has, of course, less textual

41

authority than N1, and is not free from errors of its own; e.g., in the line

Only you can hear and see (D 3, 8: ND 3, 12)

the typing error in B1, 'hear and hear', is corrected by Dylan in N1 to 'hear and see', but remains uncorrected in N2.

Although N2 was compiled with a view to publication, the text actually published by New Directions as the first American edition was that of the first English edition, edited by Dr Daniel Jones (with some very slight variants). The American edition also varied from the English edition in giving the cast of the stage-reading on 14th May 1953, in place of the cast of the B.B.C. broadcast production on 24th January 1954.

I had been in correspondence with Ruthven Todd after Dylan's death, and he sent me from New York a completely revised version of the script of the October stage-readings, containing Dylan's corrections and additions, including the extra page in the evening sequence. Meanwhile there had been a considerable demand within the B.B.C. for copies of the duplicated script (B1); so it became necessary to type and duplicate another script (B2) in which I incorporated the New York additions. Looking back, I think I ought then to have radically revised the manuscript for broadcasting, restoring the radio elements and deleting the narrative insertions; but at the time I did not realize the extent of the alterations involved in the stage-readings; and I was also respectfully reluctant to alter any of Dylan's words—though in rehearsal I had little hesitation in making two major cuts.

One reason for the demand for scripts was a question of censorship. The B.B.C. system leaves censorship to the head of the department, who can take all relevant circumstances into consideration and accepts responsibility for his decision. Laurence Gilliam as Head of Features Department was wholeheartedly in favour of broadcasting *Under Milk Wood* without alteration. The

Controller of Third Programme, on the other hand, had no powers of censorship, but was entitled to cancel the broadcast entirely if he thought it would cause offence. It was highly probable, in the climate of 1954, that *Under Milk Wood* would upset a number of listeners and expose the Third Programme to sanctimonious attack from the Press. I had a telephone call myself from a national newspaper, enquiring whether the children singing the songs would be in the studio during the rehearsals; with the clear implication that innocent children should not be exposed to the immoral influences of Llareggub.

The script of *Under Milk Wood* was accordingly referred to the Director General of the B.B.C., who ruled that it should be broadcast as scheduled, and that censorship should be left as usual to the departmental head. In appreciation of this mark of confidence, Gilliam made a couple of small token cuts, frivolously described as 'two tits and a bum' (six words in D 43, 27–28: ND 48, 24–25, and seven in D 78, 11–12: ND 86, 12).

On 15th and 16th January 1954, Dr Daniel Jones and I recorded the children's songs at Laugharne School, together with some sound effects such as Organ Morgan playing the organ. The rehearsals were scheduled for five days from Wednesday, 20th January to Sunday, 24th January, with the recording on the Sunday afternoon. As Richard Burton was rehearsing at the Old Vic every weekday, I prerecorded his narration on the Sunday before, so that I could use the discs for rehearsal until he could attend the final rehearsal and recording on Sunday, 24th January. His foster-father, Philip Burton, took the part of the Reverend Eli Jenkins.

Dr Daniel Jones attended some of the rehearsals in his dual capacity of composer and literary trustee. An unexpected difficulty arose. The first script (B1), sent to him in December, contained neither the Gossamer Beynon passage marked 'Out for Tenby' (see p. 100) nor the word 'holy' in the line 'Bless us this night, I pray'. The second script (B2), used in rehearsal, of course

43

included both. Because they had been deleted in the manuscript without a restoring *stet*, Dr Jones refused to allow them to be included in the broadcast performance. I urged that they were in Dylan's revised New York script, of which I had the copy sent me by Ruthven Todd; that the Gossamer Beynon passage was essential in order to explain why the children were singing 'hey ding a ding' behind Polly Garter's song (D 56, 7–12: ND 62, 17–22); that Dylan's ink deletion of the pencil note 'Out for Tenby' clearly implied that he intended to restore the passage: and that to omit 'holy' destroyed the metrical scheme of the Sunset Poem. Dr Jones was adamant. He would not accept any evidence other than Dylan's manuscript, which was in my possession. As literary trustee, his power was absolute. So I had no option but to instruct the cast to make the cuts accordingly. As will be seen, this was not the end of the matter.

Oddly (and fortunately) enough, nobody at the time noticed that the evidence for the long section in the evening sequence (D 81, 3–82, 27: ND 89, 9–91, 8) also depended solely on the New York script sent by Ruthven Todd. This section therefore remained in the broadcast production, and subsequently in the published text (D).

In addition to the censored lines, two passages were cut in the course of rehearsals. The first was the *Guide-Book* (D 23: ND 25–26), which I felt was out of key with the narration (though I found it visually quite effective in the stage production a couple of years later). The second cut was Mr Waldo's Song; I found that this three-minute song, delightful in itself, stopped the action and completely destroyed the dramatic tension of the closing five minutes. If Dylan had lengthened the evening sequence with 'More Stuff for Actors to Say', Mr Waldo's Song would probably have fallen more smoothly into place. I made one other alteration, involving the lines:

GOSSAMER BEYNON: At last, my love,

1ST VOICE: sighs Gossamer Beynon. And the bushy tail wags rude and ginger. (D 16, 16–20: ND 18, 13–17)

44

In MS, this passage followed the line:
the Women's Welfare hoofing, bloomered, in the
moon.   (D 17, 5: ND 19, 3–4)

As I felt that Organ Morgan's intervening speech might
confuse the listener, I switched the Gossamer Beynon
passage to follow the lines:
a small rough ready man with a bushy tail, winking in
a paper carrier.[1]   (D 16, 15: ND 18, 2)

The final rehearsal, with Richard Burton as FIRST VOICE,
took place on the Sunday morning; the production was
recorded in the afternoon. Several members of the cast
and I then went down to the Globe Theatre, to take part
in *Homage to Dylan Thomas*. This programme of poetry,
drama and music included a stage-reading of a twenty-
five-minute extract from *Under Milk Wood*, for which we
had a short rehearsal on stage before the performance
began at 8.0 p.m. The B.B.C. production was broadcast
in the Third Programme on the following evening, 25th
January. It aroused such enthusiasm among listeners and
critics that no voices of protest could be heard. By
arrangement with the B.B.C. and Dylan's trustees, the
B.B.C. production was issued as a commercial recording
by the Argo Record Company, and is therefore referred
to as A. All the actors and actresses in the B.B.C. cast
signed away their rights in this recording for the benefit
of Dylan's widow and children.

---

[1] See footnote on p. 62.

THE PUBLISHED TEXTS

After Dylan's death in November 1953 the editing of *Under Milk Wood* for publication was entrusted by J. M. Dent & Sons Ltd to Dr Daniel Jones, who, as literary trustee, would have access to the available manuscripts: including, of course, the script delivered by Dylan to the B.B.C., on which the broadcast script (B2) was based. Referring to this script, Dr Jones wrote to me at the B.B.C. on 10th January 1954:

> In the preparation of the definitive edition of *Under Milk Wood* the editorial work will of course require judgment, but this cannot even begin until all the holographs extant are collated together. In the meantime, the text you have, Text A, is backed by some degree of authenticity.

This was undeniably the proper course for an editor to take; and in the report of an interview with Dr Jones and a fellow trustee, printed in the *South Wales Evening Post* on 21st September 1956 (the day after the West End production of *Under Milk Wood*), it was stated that:

> Dr Jones, the poet's executor, gave *Under Milk Wood* its final shape. He found the script in many fragments among a mass of papers which Dylan Thomas left, on his sudden and tragic death in America. Six months of painstaking work were needed to piece it together.

It is therefore the more surprising that, apart from variations in spelling and punctuation, the published text, D and ND, is identical with the text of my B.B.C. script, B2 (including the switching of Gossamer Beynon's 'At last, my love'): except that the title of the hymn-tune

46

'Aberystwyth' is altered to 'Bread of Heaven' (D 33, 20, 22: ND 37, 17, 20), and both the word 'holy' and the passage on Gossamer Beynon (see p. 43) are omitted. This edition (D) was published by J. M. Dent & Sons Ltd on 5th March 1954: 'Llareggub' being printed throughout as 'Llaregyb'. The American edition (ND), which is almost identical with D except for the retention of 'Llareggub', was published by New Directions in New York on 28th April 1954. Meanwhile, abridged versions had been printed in the February issue of *Mademoiselle* (referred to as M), and in two issues of *The Observer* for 7th and 14th February. The abridged version in *The Observer* is based entirely on D, and has no textual significance. The version in *Mademoiselle*, however, though incomplete, is of importance. A note at the end of the text states that:

The week before Dylan Thomas went to the hospital he gave us his latest revisions in *Under Milk Wood* and a few cuts (mainly the character of Cherry Owen). We were to let him know if we wanted more. The tragedy of his death, however, prevented our asking him to cut further, and we have broken a precedent in publishing so long a manuscript. Elizabeth Reitell, who was in charge of staging the première and subsequent three performances of *Under Milk Wood*, has been a most valuable source of help in checking the manuscript.

The cuts in M amount to just under one-sixth of the complete text. M for the most part confirms N1; some spellings are Americanized, and words possibly unfamiliar to American readers are altered (e.g. 'neutered' for 'doctored'; 'spaniels' for 'corgies').

The first stage-production, produced by Henry Sherek and directed by Edward Burnham [1] and myself,

---

[1] Edward Burnham had also directed a private performance at a R.A.D.A. matinée in 1955.

opened at the Theatre Royal, Newcastle-on-Tyne, on 13th August 1956, and at the Edinburgh Festival on Tuesday, 21st August. For the stage-production, I conflated the First and Second Voices into a single Narrator (played by Donald Houston) and switched the sequence of a few speeches to facilitate the doubling of parts. Dr Jones had meanwhile resigned from his trusteeship; David Higham then became literary trustee, and raised no objection to my including the Gossamer Beynon passage and the word 'holy'. From Edinburgh, the production was taken to Liverpool, Swansea and Cardiff before opening in the West End at the New Theatre on 20th September 1956. Here it ran for seven months, until 27th April 1957. I subsequently directed the first New York production, which opened on Broadway at the Henry Miller Theatre on 15th October 1957.

In due course, J. M. Dent & Sons Ltd published an acting edition (DA) incorporating all revisions, stage movements, effects, lighting cues, etc., taken from the prompt copy of our production. Dr Jones, as editor, refused to include in this text the Gossamer Beynon passage or the word 'holy'. As a compromise, it was agreed that they should be printed in footnotes; the additional pages of text (D 81, 3–82, 27: ND 89, 9–91, 8) in the evening sequence, being similarly based on N1, will also be found in a footnote.

SUMMARY OF VERSIONS CITED

BO *Botteghe Oscure:* Quaderno IX, Rome, 1952.

  Llareggub: *A Piece for Radio Perhaps*. Incomplete radio script slightly revised for publication. Text as written by October 1951, ending at D 43, 6: ND 48, 5: lacking some sections, but containing some discarded passages not available elsewhere.

C Caedmon Publishers: New York, 1954.
  L.P. Recording TC 2005.

  Under Milk Wood. First completed text, as recorded at the YM-YWHA stage-reading in New York on 14th May 1953, under the direction of Dylan Thomas and with his participation as FIRST VOICE and THE REVEREND ELI JENKINS. Incorporating BO (with additions and revisions). C is valuable for dramatic interpretation, tempo, intonation, pronunciation, etc. Some Americanization.

MS Script delivered to B.B.C. by Dylan Thomas, 15th October 1953. Consisting of:

  (i) Manuscript of fair copy (with some rewriting), pages numbered 1 to 23.

  (ii) Typescript draft, overlapping pages numbered 20 to 51, in form of radio script, but used as part of production script for stage-readings in New York in May, 1953, and containing (*a*) textual revisions, (*b*) additional text, (*c*) alterations, additions and production notes for stage-readings, (*d*) some deletions for solo readings at Tenby, (*e*) some restorations for radio production.

(iii) Manuscript insertions of the Sunset Poem and Mr Waldo's Song.

MS provides (occasionally in deleted passages) the basic source of the unbowdlerized text as originally conceived for radio and for a non-American audience.

B1　First B.B.C. duplicated script, transcribed from MS. Not edited.

With some minor typing errors and omissions leading to variants in later versions.

N1　Copy of B1 used by Dylan Thomas for stage-readings in New York on 14th and 28th May 1953.

Containing textual corrections and revisions and additional text [1]: with some bowdlerization, Americanization and other alterations for stage-reading. N1 is the main final source for the text, but with a bias towards American stage-reading and against dramatic production in radio or theatre.

N2　Copy of B1 edited by Ruthven Todd and Elizabeth Reitell from scripts of New York stage-readings (mainly N1).

N2 is useful for clarifying doubtful corrections in N1. It does not add anything to the text of N1, but has slight errors and omissions of its own.

B2　Second B.B.C. duplicated script, edited and transcribed from MS.

Incorporating additional material from a copy of N2.

A　Argo Record Company, 1954. L.P. Recording RG 21/22.

Recording of B.B.C. broadcast of 25th January

---

[1] Dylan's manuscript of the additional text (D 81, 3—82, 27: ND 89, 9—91, 8) was presented by Miss Reitell to Yale University Library.

1954: using text of B2, but with three major and three minor omissions. The original B.B.C. recording (from which A was taken) was processed and is retained in B.B.C. Recorded Programmes Library Archives with the number LP 24171.

M *Mademoiselle*, New York, February 1954.

Abridged version, containing approximately five-sixths of the text. Based on N1, slightly revised and abridged by Dylan Thomas. Some bowdlerization and Americanization. M, though incomplete, is valuable as a final version of N1, particularly in confirming punctuation.

D J. M. Dent & Sons Ltd. First published edition, edited by Dr Daniel Jones, 1954.

D is the standard text, nearly identical with B2, but with two significant omissions (see pp. 100 and 116).

ND New Directions. First American edition, edited by Dr Daniel Jones, 1954.

Text almost identical with D.

DA J. M. Dent & Sons Ltd. Acting Edition, edited by Dr Daniel Jones, 1958.

Incorporating revisions of text and alterations of sequence by Douglas Cleverdon for the Edinburgh Festival stage-production, 1956.

N3 A duplicated script, quarto, apparently based upon a conflation of C, N1 and ND, contains transcripts by Kenn Mileston of some New York notes by Dylan Thomas, a few of which do not appear to be recorded elsewhere. When quoted, these notes are cited N3.

The abridged version in two successive issues of *The Observer* on 7th and 14th February 1954, based on D, with illustrations by John Minton, and the abridged version, based on B2, submitted by the B.B.C. for the Italia Prize in 1954, have no textual significance.

ANALYSIS OF TEXTUAL VARIANTS

D and ND, the versions published respectively by J. M. Dent & Sons Ltd in London and by New Directions in New York in 1954, are taken as the standard texts. In the page-and-line references, page numbers are printed in 'modern' figures (0123456789), line-numbers in 'old style' (0123456789). Main entries (from D and ND) are ranged to the left; variants are indented, with abbreviations for cited versions ranged to the right.

In each main entry, the name of the character is printed in small capitals. In quotations of variants, the name of the character is printed in lower-case italic, regardless of the setting in the version cited. Where D and ND differ, the D variant is given in the main entry; the ND variant is then given below it.

Notes in square brackets normally refer to the preceding word or phrase or sentence, except when they clearly refer to a production note.

Within the square brackets, a word deleted from a text is printed in roman or italic in accordance with the text; the explanatory textual note is printed in italic.

Where a textual variant is uniform throughout a version, the first occurrence only is specified, with the note [*sic throughout*].

When a sequence of several consecutive versions (in the order given in the Summary) contains the same textual variant, only the first and last versions are cited, with — between them. Thus MS—B2 represents MS B1 N1 N2 B2.

Variants in punctuation, indentation and spacing are noted only when they may affect emphasis and timing in dramatic production. Obvious misprints, typing errors and spelling mistakes are not usually noted, unless they are of some interest or significance.

A quoted variant usually contains only enough words or punctuation to enable it to be clearly identified by reference to the main entry.

A line may be *deleted* intentionally (as in N1 by Dylan Thomas for American audience), *omitted* intentionally (as in M, abridged by Dylan Thomas), or *not in* (because not yet written, as in BO).

D.T. = Dylan Thomas, D.C. = Douglas Cleverdon.

D 1, 17: ND 1, 17
the undertaker and the fancy woman,
    the barber and the fancy woman,   BO

D 1, 17–19: ND 1, 17–19
the fancy woman, drunkard, dressmaker, preacher, policeman, the webfoot cocklewomen
    the fancy woman, the webfoot cocklewomen
    [*four words omitted through typing error*]   B1
    [B1 *not corrected*]   N1 N2 M

D1, 22: ND 1, 22
Down the aisles of the organplaying wood.
    Down aisles of   BO

D 1, 24: ND 2, 1
the jollyrodgered sea
    the jolly, rodgered sea   BO MS M
    the jolly-rodgered sea   B1 N1
    the jolly rodgered sea   N2 B2 DA

D 2, 6: ND 2, 9
Only *your* eyes are unclosed to see
    Only your eyes   MS—B2 M
    unclosed, to see   BO MS

D 2, 10: ND 2, 14
the *Skylark, Zanzibar,*
    the Skylark, Phoebe and Sally and Mary Ann,
    Zanzibar   BO C

D 2, 15
Llaregyb
    Llareggub [*sic throughout*]   BO—M ND
    Llaregyb [*sic throughout*]   D DA

D 2, 17: ND 2, 20
Listen. It is night in the chill, squat chapel, hymning in
bonnet
    in the squat, locked chapel, hymning, in bonnet BO

D 2, 17–28: ND 2, 20–31
Listen [*to*] snuggeries of babies.
    [*Omitted*]   M

D 2, 20: ND 2, 24:
night in the four-ale, quiet as a domino;
    night in the four-ale bar, quiet as a domino;   C

D 2, 21: ND 2, 24–25
in Ocky Milkman's lofts
    in Ocky's lofts   BO
    in Ocky Milkman's loft [s *deleted*]   N1
    in Ocky Milkman's loft   DA

D 2, 23: ND 2, 26
like black flour. It is to-night
    like black flour. Listen. It is to-night   BO C

D 2, 27: ND 2, 30
and rosy tin teacaddy. It is night
    and rosy tin teacaddy, it is night   BO

D 2, 32: ND 3, 3
by the Sailors Arms
    by the Sailors' Arms [*sic throughout*]   BO MS—B2 M

D 3, 4: ND 3, 7
salt and silent black, bandaged night.
    silent, black, bandaged   BO

D 3, 5–6: ND 3, 8–9
in the blinded bedrooms, the combs and petticoats over
the chairs
    all the combs   BO
    combs [*wrongly pronounced as if hair-combs: should
    be cŏmbs, short for* combinations]   C A

D 3, 9: ND 3, 12
Only you can hear and see,
    can hear and hear, [*typing error*]   B1
    [*Not corrected*]   N2 M
    can hear and [hear *deleted*] see [*inserted*]   N1

D 3, 22–23: ND 3, 25–27
where the fish come biting out and nibble him down to
his wishbone, and the long drowned nuzzle up to him.
    come biting out like finned and lightning bugs from
    behind the wet green wallpaper of the undersea and
    nibble him   BO
    come biting out from behind the wet green wallpaper
    of the undersea and nibble him   C
    come biting out [like bugs from behind the wet green
    wallpaper of the undersea *deleted*] and nibble him MS
    down to his wishbone [comma *deleted*] and   N1 N2
    down to his wishbone and the long drowned   M
    and the long drowned nuzzle up to him . . .
                                   MS—N2 M
D 4, 1: ND 4, 5
SECOND DROWNED
    [*Production note*] (Dylan take)   N1

D 4, 17: ND 4, 22
FIFTH DROWNED
    [*Production note*] Dyl take   N1

D 4, 23: ND 5, 4
Tell my missus no I never
    no my never   MS B1 B2
    no [my *altered to*] I never   N1 N2

D 4, 27: ND 5, 8
Yes they did.
    Yes, they did.   BO MS—B2 M ND

D 5, 7: ND 5, 15
Is there rum and laverbread?
    and lavabread?   BO MS—B2 M ND

D 6, 2: ND 6, 14
How's the tenors in Dowlais?
    the tenor   B1—B2 M

D 6, 12–13: ND 7, 2–3
From where you are you can hear in Cockle Row in the
spring, moonless night,
    From where you are, you can hear, in Cockle Row
                       BO MS—B2 M
    Cockle Row, in   BO
    the spring, moonless, night   B1 N1 N2 M
    [*Production note*] quicker   N1

D 6, 13–14: ND 7, 3–4
Miss Price, dressmaker and sweetshop-keeper, dream of
    Miss Price, dressmaker, dream of   BO

D 6, 18: ND 7, 8
barnacle-breasted, flailing up the cockles
    barnacle-breasted flailing up   BO MS—B2 M

D 6, 28: ND 7, 18
merino, tussore, cretonne, crepon
    merino, shantung, tussore, cretonne, crepon   BO

D 7, 3: ND 7, 22
your Welsh wool knitted jacket,
    your Welsh wool knitted jacket twelve and eleven
    three,   BO

56

D 7, 12–13: ND 8, 4–5
before the mice gnaw at your bottom drawer will you say
    your bottom drawer, will you say   BO

D 7, 19: ND 8, 11
Noise of money-tills and chapel bells
    (*The noise of money-tills and bells*)   BO
    [*Line deleted, presumably for stage reading. Produc-*
    tion note] No sound effects here   N1
    [*Line deleted*]   N2
    [*Line omitted*]   C M
    [*Sound effect of chiming money-tills*]   A

D 7, 30–31: ND 8, 22–23
driving out the bare bold girls
    the bare, bold girls   BO MS—B2 M

D 8, 1–2: ND 8, 24–25
JACK BLACK (*Loudly*) Ach y fi!
    Jack Black: Ach y fi!   BO

D 8, 4–15: ND 9, 1–12
FIRST VOICE [*to*] currants.
    [*Not in*]   BO C

D 8, 6: ND 9, 3
SECOND VOICE
    [*2nd Voice deleted*] Evans the Death [*inserted as*
    speaker]   N1

D 8, 8–9: ND 9, 5–6
snow lie deep on the goosefield.
    grassfield [*typing error*]   B1
    [grassfield *altered to*] greenfield [1]   N1
    greenfield   N2 M

---

[1] *In correcting 'grassfield' to 'greenfield', D.T. presumably forgot the original 'goosefield'.*

D 8, 10–11: ND 9, 7–8
making welsh-cakes in the snow,
Welshcakes   MS—B2 M

D 8, 13–14: ND 9, 11
while his mother dances in the snow kitchen
    dances [cross as two sticks *deleted*] in the snow
    kitchen   MS

D 8, 17–18: ND, 9 14–15
next to the undertaker's, lie, alone,
    next to the cobbler's lie, alone,   BO C

D 8, 19–20: ND 9, 16–17
Mister Waldo, rabbitcatcher, barber, herbalist, cat-
doctor, quack, his fat pink hands, palms up,
    Mister Waldo, dentist, barber, herbalist, his fat pink
    hands, palms up,   BO

D 8, 23–24: ND 9, 20–21
a slice of cold bread pudding under the pillow;
    of old bread pudding   MS B1 B2
    [old *altered to*] cold   N1 N2

D 10, 10: ND 11, 12
He hasn't got a log
    He hasn't got a leg   BO—M ND DA

D 10, 22: ND 12, 2
Oh it makes my heart bleed
    Oh, it makes my heart bleed   BO MS—B2 M

D 11, 13: ND 12, 19
WIFE (*Tearfully*) . . . Oh, Waldo, Waldo!
    Wife: Oh, Waldo, Waldo!   BO

D 11, 15: ND 12, 21
MR WALDO
    Mister Waldo: [*sic throughout*]   BO

D 11, 16: ND 12, 22
I'm *widower* Waldo now.
    [*Production note*] *more enjoyment*   N1

D 12, 12: ND 13, 23
Playing mwchins
    Playing moochins   MS—B2 M

D 12, 23: ND 14, 11
ANOTHER MOTHER
    First Woman: BO
    Matti's Mother: DA

D 12, 24: ND 14, 12
Waldo, Wal-do! what you doing with our Matti?
    what are you doing   C

D 13, 7: ND 14, 19
FIRST WOMAN
    Second Woman: BO
    Matti's Mother: DA

D 13, 11: ND 15, 1
SECOND WOMAN
    Third Woman: BO
    Fourth Neighbour: DA

D 13, 13: ND 15, 3
THIRD WOMAN
    Fourth Woman: BO
    Third Neighbour: DA

D 13, 14: ND 15, 4
Effie Bevan
    Effie Beynon   BO

D 13, 15: ND 15, 5
FOURTH WOMAN
    Fifth Woman: BO
    Fourth Neighbour: DA

D 13, 17: ND 15, 7
FIFTH WOMAN
   Sixth Woman: BO
   First Neighbour: DA

D 13, 23: ND 15, 13
LITTLE BOY
   Child: BO

D 14, 2–3: ND 15, 16–17
Now, in her iceberg-white, holily laundered crinoline
nightgown,
   holily laundered organdie nightgown,   BO

D 14, 6: ND 15, 20
Mrs Ogmore-Pritchard widow,
   Mrs Ogmore-Pritchard, widow,   BO MS—B2 M ND

D 14, 7: ND 15, 21
Mr Ogmore, linoleum, retired, and Mr Pritchard,
   Mr Ogmore linoleum retired and Mr Pritchard, BO

D 14, 8: ND 15, 22
failed bookmaker, who maddened by besoming,
   who, maddened   BO
   who. maddened [*comma probably intended*]   MS

D 14, 8–11: ND 15, 22–25
swabbing and scrubbing, the voice of the vacuum cleaner
and the fume of polish, ironically swallowed disinfectant,
   swabbing and scrubbing, mopping and gimping, the
   voice of the vacuum cleaner and the fume of polish,
   swallowed disinfectant,   BO

D 14, 18: ND 16, 7
MR OGMORE
   Mr Ogmore: [*fearfully   deleted*]   N1 MS

D 14, 19: ND 16, 8
Oh, Mrs Ogmore!
    [*Production note*] no sniffing   N1

D 14, 20: ND 16, 9
MR PRITCHARD
    Mr Pritchard: [*grieving   deleted*]   MS

D 14, 21: ND 16, 10
Oh, Mrs Pritchard!
    [*Production note*] quicker   N1

D 14, 24: ND 16, 13
Tell me your tasks, in order.
    Tell me your tasks in order.   BO

D 14, 26–16, 5: ND 16, 15–18, 2
I must put my pyjamas [*to*] and then I must raise them.
    [*No full points at end of sentences throughout this
    sequence*]   BO

D 15, 4: ND 16, 22
I must dress behind the curtain
    [*Production note above this line in top margin*]
    More pain   N1

D 16, 9–20, 6: ND 18, 6–22, 15
FIRST VOICE [*to*] My foxy darling.
    [*Not in*]   BO

D 16, 13: ND 18, 10
chintz curtains and a three-pieced suite,
    a three-piece suite,   MS
    a three-pieced suite, [*typing error*]   B1
    (*Not corrected by D.T.*)   N1

61

D 16, 16–20: ND 18, 13–17
GOSSAMER BEYNON [*to*] And the bushy tail wags rude and
ginger.
   [*These lines* [1] *follow* D 17, 5: ND 19, 4
   bloomered in the moon]   C MS—N2 M

D 16, 23: ND 18, 20
SECOND VOICE
   1st Voice   C

D 17, 1: ND 18, 25
P.C. Attila Rees has got his truncheon out
   Police Constable Atilla Evans   C
   P.C. Atilla Rees [*sic throughout*]   MS—M

D 17, 4–5: ND 19, 3–4
the Women's Welfare hoofing, bloomered, in the moon.
   [*Followed by* D 16, 16–20: ND 18, 13–17]
                                          C MS—N2 M
D 17, 7: ND 19, 6
Mrs and Mrs Floyd, the cocklers,
   Mr and Mrs Curly Floyd, the cocklers,   C

D 17, 9: ND 19, 8
toothless, salt and brown,
   toothless, salt, and brown,   MS

---

[1] *For the first B.B.C. radio production (embodied in* B2
and A) *these lines were transferred to follow the narration
ending '* a small rough ready man with a bushy tail winking
in a paper carrier'. *The intention was to link Gossamer
Beynon's '* At last, my love,' *more closely with the rough
ready man and thus to identify her more clearly for the
listener. For the stage production, it would have been
better to restore the original sequence and thus to allow
a lapse of time for the climax of Gossamer's amorous
dream.*

D 17, 11–18, 4: ND 19, 10–20, 4
And high above [*to*] He drinks the fish.
[*Omitted*]   M

D 17, 18: ND 19, 17
MRS UTAH WATKINS (*Bleating*)
Mrs Utah Watkins: MS—B2

D 17, 21: ND 19, 20
Pass the slipstitch over . . .
   Pass the slipstitch over . . .
   (*Mrs Utah Watkins bleats*)   C MS—B2

D 17, 22–19, 25: ND 19, 21–22, 6
Ocky Milkman [*to*] owlmeat, dogs' eyes, manchop.
   [*In the stage production, scene changes necessitated
   the switching of sequences as follows:
   Willy Nilly (D 18, 16–24: ND 20, 16–24)
   P.C. Atilla Rees (D 18, 6–14: ND 20, 6–14)
   Sinbad Sailors, Lily Smalls, Mae Rose Cottage,
   Bessie Bighead (D 18, 26–19, 21: ND 21, 2–26)
   Ocky Milkman, Cherry Owen (D 17, 23–18, 4:
   ND 19, 22–20, 4)
   Butcher Beynon (D 19, 22: ND 21, 27)*]   DA

D 18, 5–6: ND 20, 5–6
FIRST VOICE
P.C. Attila Rees lumps out of bed,
   1st Voice: P.C. Atilla Rees
   Atilla Rees: [*inserted as speaker*] lumps out of bed,
                                                      N1
D 18, 5–15: ND 20, 5–14
FIRST VOICE [*to*] His helmet swashes in the dark.
   [*Not in*]   C

D 18, 6–7: ND 20, 6–7
dead to the dark and still foghorning,
   dead to the dark, and still foghorning,   MS—B2
63

D 18, 10: ND 20, 10
A VOICE (*Murmuring*)
Attila (*murmuring*)   DA

D 18, 12: ND 20, 12
FIRST VOICE
[*1st voice altered to*] Atilla Rees: N1 N2

D 18, 16–28: ND 20, 16–21, 4
walks fourteen miles [*to*] Gossamer Beynon.
    walks fourteen miles and delivers the post in his
    dream as he does every night. Sinbad Sailors hugs
    his pillow called Gossamer Beynon.   C

D 18, 18: ND 20, 18
rat-a-tats hard and sharp on Mrs Willy Nilly.
    [*spacing-sign after* sharp. *Production note*]
    space more   N1

D 19, 4–12: ND 21, 9–17
Mrs Rose Cottage's eldest [*to*] in the stories.
    Mrs Rose Cottage's eldest, Mae is dreaming of
    tall . . . tower . . . white . . . furnace . . . cave . . .
    flower . . . ferret . . . waterfall . . . sigh . . . without
    any words at all.   C
    Mrs Rose- [*hyphen inserted: sic throughout*] Cottage's
                                                              N1 N2
D 19, 4: ND 21, 9
Mrs Rose Cottage's eldest, Mae, peals off her pink-and-
white skin
    Mae, peels off   MS B2 M
    [peals *typing error in* B1, *corrected to*] peals   N1 N2

D 19, 8: ND 21, 13
the burning tall hollow splashes of leaves
    sploshes [*typing error*]   B1 N2
    [sploshes *corrected to*] splashes   N1

64

D 19, 14–15: ND 21, 19–20
Bessie Bighead, hired help, born in the workhouse,
  [*Footnote*] For American audiences: read 'poor-
  house' for 'workhouse'.   DA

D 19, 16–17: ND 21, 21–22
snores bass and gruff on a couch of straw in a loft in Salt
Lake Farm and picks a posy
  snores bass-baritone in Utah Watkins' attic and
  picks a posy   C

D 19, 25: ND 22, 4
owlmeat, dogs' eyes, manchop.
  owl meat   MS—N2 M ND
  owlmeat   D DA
  [*Production note*] Flatter   N1

D 19, 27–20, 2: ND 22, 6–11
Mr Beynon [*to*] wild giblets.
  [*Not in*]   C

D 20, 2: ND 22, 11
hunting on pigback shoots down the wild giblets.
  Shoot [s *added in pencil, probably by D.C. as
  producer*]   MS
  giblets. Bang! Bang!! [*added for stage effect*]   DA

D 20, 10: ND 22, 19
SECOND VOICE
  [*Deleted*]   N1 N2
  [*Omitted*]   M

D 20, 17: ND 23, 1
FIRST VOICE
  [*Corrected to*] 2nd Voice: N1 N2
  2nd Voice   M

65

D 20, 22–22, 6: ND 23, 6–24, 25

the Reverend Eli Jenkins, poet, preacher [*to*] In Donkey
Street, so furred with sleep,
> Mr Eli Jenkins, poet, preacher, Organ Morgan,
> organist, butcher Beynon, Mr Pugh schoolteacher,
> and Mary Ann Sailors turn in their deep towards-
> dawn sleep and dream of
> *Reverend Eli Jenkins:* Eisteddfodau
> *Organ Morgan:* Oratorio
> *Butcher Beynon:* Fishing for puffins
> *Mr Pugh:* Murder
> *Mary Ann Sailors:* The River of Jordan
> *1st Voice:* In Donkey Street, so furred with sleep,
>
> BO

> Mr Eli Jenkins, poet, preacher, Mrs Organ Morgan,
> groceress, Butcher Beynon, Mr Pugh schoolteacher,
> and Mary Ann Sailors turn in their deep towards-
> dawn sleep and dream of
> *Mrs Organ Morgan:* Silence
> *Reverend Eli Jenkins:* Eisteddfodau
> *Butcher Beynon:* Fishing for puffins
> *Mr Pugh:* Murder
> *Mary Ann Sailors:* The River of Jordan
> *1st Voice:* In Donkey Street, so furred with sleep,
>
> C

D 20, 26: ND 23, 10

Eisteddfodau.
> [Eisteddfodau *the correct spelling in* B1, *was altered
> in* N1 *by D.T. to* Eistedfoddau *and then re-corrected
> by him*] Eisteddfodau stet   N1
> [Eisteddfodau *was incorrectly altered in* N2 *to two
> words*] Eisted foddau   N2

D 20, 27–30: ND 23, 11–14

SECOND VOICE [*to*] a beer-tent black with parchs.
> [*These lines omitted*]   M
> [parchs *altered to*] preachers   N1 N2

66

[*Footnote*] For American audiences: for 'parchs'
read 'preachers'.   DA

D 21, 2: ND 23, 16
Mr Pugh, schoolmaster, fathoms asleep,
    [fathoms *corrected to*] fast asleep,   N1 N2

D 21, 4–6: ND 23, 18–20
and psst! whistles up
MR PUGH
Murder.
    [*altered to*] and
    Mr Pugh: Psst!
    1st Voice: whistles up
    Mr Pugh: Murder.   N1 N2
    [*as altered in* N1]   M DA

D 21, 28: ND 24, 17
ducking under the gippo's clothespegs,
    [gippo's *altered to*] gypsies' clothespegs   N1 N2 M
    [*Footnote*] For American audiences: for 'gippo's'
    read 'gypsies'.'   DA

D 22, 7: ND 24, 26
Polly Garter, Nogood Boyo,
    Polly Garter, Cherry Owen soak, Nogood Boyo,

                                                 BO

D 22, 8: ND 24, 27
and dream of
    [*Production note*] (joy)   N3

D 22, 10: ND 25, 2
Harems.
    [*Altered to*] Turkish girls. Horizontal.   N1 N2
    Turkish girls. Horizontal.   M

D 22, 12: ND 25, 4
Babies.
    Polly Garter: Babies.
    Cherry Owen: The Devil.   BO

D 22, 21: ND 25, 13
One distant bell-note, faintly reverberating
faintly reverberating on BO MS—B2 M

D 22, 24–26: ND 25, 16–18
high, cool, and green, and from this small circle of
stones,[1] made not by druids but by Mrs Beynon's Billy,
you can see all the town
high, cool, and green. From it you can see M

D 22, 26–30: ND 25, 18–22
all the town below you sleeping in the first of the dawn.
[*to*] The town ripples like a lake in the waking haze.
the first of the dawn. The hill grazes on the lower
fields, and the fields go down to the hazed town,
rippling like a lake, to drink. BO C

D 22, 29: ND 25, 22
A dog barks in his sleep, farmyards away,
farmyards away [in the waking haze *deleted in ink*]
MS
[*In margin, written in pencil by D.T., and subsequently
deleted in ink; probably signifying* 'Not for Tenby'
(*see p. 37*) *and referring to Voice of Guide-Book*]
NOT FOR NOW MS

D 23, 1–11: ND 25, 23–26, 7
VOICE OF A GUIDE BOOK [*to*] by the liberal use of
[*Bracketed in pencil to bottom of p. 14 of* MS, *ending*
liberal use of. *Beside bracket, written in pencil by
D.T., and subsequently deleted in ink: probably
signifying* 'Not for Tenby'] NO MS

D 23, 1–25: ND 25, 23–26, 20
VOICE OF A GUIDE BOOK [*to*] of no architectural interest.
[*Omitted*] A

---

[1] *See pp. 32–3.*

D 23, 9: ND 26, 4
humble, two-storied houses
   humble two-storied houses   BO MS

D 23, 20: ND 26, 15–16
some of that picturesque sense of the past
   some of the picturesque sense of the past   BO

D 23, 26–28: ND 26, 21–23
A cock crows
FIRST VOICE
The principality of the sky lightens now,
   (*Cock crows*)
   1st Voice: A cock crows. The principality of the sky
                                       C
   2nd Voice (if necc.) [*inserted by D.T. before sound*
   effect] A COCK CROWS. [*signifying that sound effect*
   becomes line of narration]   N1
   The Principality of the sky   BO

D 24, 5: ND 27, 1
the chimneys' slow upflying snow
   the chimney's slow upflying snow   MS

D 24, 8: ND 27, 4
SECOND VOICE
   [*not in*]   BO C

D 24, 15–16: ND 27, 11–12
and tells them softly to empty Coronation Street
   tells them, softly, to   BO MS—B2 M

D 24, 20; ND 27, 17
Towns lovelier than ours,
   lovlier   MS B1
   [*corrected to*] lov'lier   N1 N2
   lov'lier   M

D 24, 28: ND 27, 24
Or Moel yr Wyddfa's glory
  Moel y Wyddfa's   BO—N2 M

D 24, 29: ND 27, 25
Carnedd Llewelyn beauty born,
  Carnedd Llewellyn   MS—N2 M

D 25, 2: ND 27, 28
By Penmaenmawr defiant,
  Penmaen Mawr   BO MS—B2 M

D 25, 3
Llaregyb Hill a molehill seems,
  Llareggub Hill   ND
  Llarreggub *Hill*, [*poem printed in italic*]   BO
  Llareggub Hill   MS—B2 M

D 25, 5: ND 28, 3
By Sawdde, Senny, Dovey, Dee
  Sawdde, Senni   BO MS—B2 M
  Sawdde, Senny   D DA
  Sawddwy, Senny   ND

D 25, 8: ND 26, 6
Llyfnant with its waterfall,
  Llynfant   BO—B2 M

D 25, 9: ND 28, 7
Claerwen, Cleddau, Dulais, Daw,
  Dulas, Daw,   BO—B2 M

D 25, 10: ND 28, 8
Ely, Gwili, Ogwr, Nedd,
  Ned,   BO—B2 M

D 25, 11: ND 28, 9
Small is our River Dewi, Lord
  our *River Dewi*,   BO MS—B2 M

70

D 25, 13: ND 28, 11
By Carreg Cennen, King of time,
Cerig Cennin,   BO—B2 M

D 25, 13–14: ND 28, 11–12
By Carreg Cennen [*to*] Our Heron Head
By Cerig Cennin, King of time,
Our ruin in the spinnet
Where owls do wink and squirrels climb
Is aged but half a minute.

By Strumble or by Dinas Head,
Our *Heron Head*   BO C

D 25, 14: ND 28, 12
Our Heron Head
Our *Heron Head*   BO MS—B2 M

D 26, 4–5: ND 29, 4–5
comes downstairs from a dream of royalty
a dream of Royalty   BO

D 26, 8: ND 29, 8
and looks at herself in Mr Beynon's shaving-glass
and looks at her face in   C BO

D 26, 11: ND 29, 11
Oh there's a face!
    [Oh, there's a face!
    There's a oil painting!
    Hair, eyes, nose, lips, everything,
    Got a little moustache as well,
    There's swank!
    These lines deleted first in pencil, then in ink, with
    query added in margin]
    Oh there's a face! [*added later in pencil*]   MS
    Oh, there's a face!   BO
71

D 26, 11–20: ND 29, 11–20
Oh there's a face [*to*] Look at your complexion!
    Oh, there's a face!
    Where you get that nose from, Lily?
    Got it from my father, silly.
    Oh, there's a conk!

    Where you get that hair from?
    Got it from an old tom cat.
    Oh, there's a perm!

    Look at your complexion!   BO

    [*as in* BO *above, except for*]
    Where d'you get that nose from, Lily?   C

D 26, 13: ND 29, 13
Got it from a old tom cat
    [*Note in margin*] a (sic)   N2

D 26, 15: ND 29, 15
Oh there's a perm!
    Oh, there's a perm!   MS—B2 M
    [*Inserted after* D 26, 15: ND 29, 15:
    What big eyes you got!
    Big as a bluebottles. [*sic*]
    Nice shade of custard too.
    Mind they don't drop out.
    These lines deleted first in pencil, then in ink, with
    query added in margin]   MS

D 26, 18: ND 29, 18
You've got it on upside down!
    [You're wearing it upside down *deleted in ink: final*
    version added in pencil]   MS

D 27, 5: ND 30, 5
Cross my heart.
    [*Production note*] Too Irish 'heart'   N1

D 27, 17: ND 30, 17
In the cat-box?
    [*Production note*] Slower   N1

D 27, 21: ND 30, 21–22
and whispers on the stairs
    and whispers on the stairs
    (*Footfalls on Creaking Stairs*)   BO

D 27, 25: ND 31, 1
I've throttled your parakeet.
    I've killed your budgerigar.   BO

D 27, 27: ND 31, 3
I've put cheese in the mouseholes.
    in the mousehole.   C

D 28, 6: ND 31, 10
Has Mr Jenkins read his poetry?
    said his poetry?   C

D 28, 9: ND 31, 14
Yes, dear.
    Yes, dear, he's indoors now.   C BO

D 28, 13: ND 31, 18
I want to see
    [*Production note*] come in quicker   N1

D 28, 18–19: ND 31, 23–24
She's tucked her dress in her bloomers—oh, the baggage!
    in her bloomers! Oh, the baggage!   BO

D 28, 21–23: ND 32, 2–4
P.C. Attila Rees, ox-broad, barge-booted, stamping out
[*to*] damp helmet . . .
    P.C. Atilla Evans, ox-broad, barge-booted, cumber-
    ing out in a heavy huff . . .   C BO
    P.C. Atilla Rees, ox-broad, barge-booted, stamping
    out of Handcuff House [in a heavy huff, glaring

under *altered to* around him from under *deleted*] in a
heavy beef-red huff, black-browed under his damp
helmet . . .   MS
Rhys [*typing* e*rror*]   B1
[*Corrected*]   N1 N2
under his helmet [1]   M

D 29, 5: ND 32, 15
Mary Ann Sailors
Mary Ann the Sailors [*see note to* D 31, 12–13: ND
34, 28–29]   BO—M

D 29, 7: ND 32, 17
MARY ANN SAILORS
Mary Ann the Sailors: MS

D 29, 12–14: ND 32, 22–25
Organ Morgan at his bedroom window playing chords
on the sill to the morning fishwife gulls who, heckling
over Donkey Street, observe
    [Organ Morgan at his bedroom window playing
    chords on the sill to *omitted*] The morning fishwife
    gulls [who *omitted*], heckling over Donkey Street,
    observe: M
    chords [to *deleted*] on the [morning *deleted*] sill to the
    morning fishwife gulls who, [crying *deleted*] heckling
    over Donkey Street, observe: MS
    who, crying over   BO

D 29, 17: ND 33, 3
buttoning my waistcoat, ping goes a button,
    buttoning my buttons, ping goes a button,   BO C

D 29, 23–27: ND 33, 9–13
Oh, Mrs Sarah, [*to*] Ta, Mrs Sarah.
    'Oh, Mrs Owen, can you spare a loaf now? There's

---

[1] '*Damp*' *was cut because the earlier reference,* '*His
helmet swashes in the dark*' (D 18, 13: ND 18, 13–14)
occurred in a sequence omitted from M.

74

no bread in the house. Nice bit of sun we've got this
morning. Thank you, fach.'   BO
Oh, Mrs Sarah, can you spare a loaf, love? There's
no bread in the house. How's your boils this
morning?   C

D 30, 2–9: ND 33, 15–22
Me, Mrs Dai Bread Two, [to] lighting up my pipe.
    Me, Mrs Dai Bread Two, gaudied to kill in a yellow
jumper, yellow petticoat, flashing sash, high heel
shoes with one heel missing, tortoiseshell comb in
my bright black tousle, nothing else, lolling at the
doorway, scowling at the sunshine, lighting up my
pipe.   BO
    Me, Mrs Dai Bread Two, gaudy to kill in a tangerine
jumper full of moth-holes, dirty yellow petticoat
above my knees, dirty pretty knees, high-heel shoes
[remainder as BO except for] lolling in the doorway,
                                                               C

D 30, 5: ND 33, 18–19
tortoiseshell comb in my bright black slinky hair,
    tortoiseshell [underlined by D.T. in pencil, with query
    in margin]   N1

D 30, 7: ND 33, 19–20
nothing else at all but a dab of scent,
    nothing else at all on [inserted] but a dab of scent,
                                                 N1 N2
    nothing else at all on but a dab of scent,   M

D 30, 17: ND 34, 2
Me, Nogood Boyo, up to no good in the wash-house.
    Me, Nogood Boyo up to no good   BO
    Me, nogood Boyo, up to no good   MS B1
    [Corrected to] Nogood   N1 N2

D 30, 24—31, 6: ND 34, 10–22
Me, Polly Garter, under the washing line, [to] Now
frying pans spit, kettles and cats purr in the kitchen.
    Me, Polly Garter, giving the breast in the garden to

my new bonny baby and listening to the voices of the
blooming birds who seem to say to me
Childrens' [*sic*] *Voices* (*singsonging, one after the
other, on different notes*)
Polly
Love
Love
Polly
I love
Polly
Polly
Loves me
Polly
Love
Love
Polly
We love Polly
And Polly love
Lovely Polly
Loves us all . . .
1st Voice: Now frying pans spit. Kettles and cats
purr in the kitchen.   BO
Me, Polly Garter, giving the breast in the garden to
my new bonny baby and listening to the voices in the
voices of the blooming birds.
1st Voice: Now frying pans spit, kettles and cats
purr in the kitchen.   C
[kitchen *corrected to*] kitchens.   N1 N2

D 30, 29–30: ND 34, 15–16
you poor little milky creature.
    milky [creature *deleted*] thing [*inserted*].   N1 N2
    milky thing.   M

D 31, 3: ND 34, 19
Single long high chord on strings
    [*altered to*] *Single long note held by Welsh male*
    voices   N1 N2
    [*As* N1]   M
76

D 31, 7–13: ND 34, 23–29

All the way down from Bay View, [*to*] swigs from the saucebottle. Mary Ann Sailors
    all the way down from Bay View to Bottom Cottage
    and Mr Waldo. Mary Ann the Sailors   M

D 31, 12–13: ND 34, 28–29

Mary Ann Sailors
    Mary Ann the Sailors [*sic henceforward in narration*]
                                 MS—M

MARY ANN SAILORS
    Mary Ann the Sailors: MS B1 B2
    [the *deleted*] [1]   N1 N2 M

D 32, 4–6: ND 35, 20–22

broods and bubbles over her coven of kettles on the hissing hot range

    covern   MS
    cavern   B1
    [cavern *corrected to*] coven   N1 N2
    on the hissing hot hob   C

D 32, 7, 11: ND 35, 23, 36, 3

FIRST VOICE
    [*altered to*] 2nd Voice: [2]   C N1

D 32, 10: ND 36, 2

finds a rhyme and dips his pen in his cocoa.
    in the cocoa.   BO

---

[1] *The usage is not consistent, but it appears that D.T. generally preferred* MARY ANN SAILORS *as the name of the character,* 'Mary Ann the Sailors' *in narration. Henceforward no variants in the text are noted.*

[2] *Presumably because in the New York readings D.T. read both* FIRST VOICE *and* REV. ELI JENKINS.

D 32, 19: ND 36, 11
blind and fine-fingered savours his sea-fry.
blind and fine-fingered flavours his sea-fry.   BO C

D 32, 20–34, 17: ND 36, 12–38, 19
FIRST VOICE: Mr and Mrs Cherry Owen in their Donkey
Street room [*to*] *Mr and Mrs Cherry Owen laugh de-
lightedly together*
    [*Not in*]   BO
    [*Omitted*]   M

D 32, 24–25: ND 36, 16–17
broth of spuds and baconrind and leeks and bones.
baconrind and bones.   C

D 32, 27–28: ND 36, 19–20
See that smudge on the wall by the picture of Auntie [1]
Blossom? That's where you threw the sago.
    See that smudge on the wall by the almanac? That's
    where you threw the gravy.   C
    dumpling [*written by D.T. above* sago *which is not
    deleted*]   N1
    dumpling [sago *deleted*]   N2

D 32, 29: ND 36, 21
Cherry Owen laughs with delight
    [*In the recorded stage reading of May 14, 1953, in New
    York, Mr and Mrs Cherry Owen laugh uproariously
    throughout the scene*]   C

---

[1] *As an instance of the allusiveness of the text of* UNDER
MILK WOOD, *one may conjecture that Auntie Blossom's
name derives, consciously or subconsciously, from* 'Cherry
Blossom Boot Polish', *famous in England since the 19th
century.*

78

D 33, 2–34, 16: ND 36, 23–38, 18
You only missed me by a inch [*to*] you snored all night
like a brewery.

> You only missed me by a inch. And remember the
> fish-bucket? Over you tumbled, flagons and all, and
> the floor was all eels, flatfish and blood.
> *Cherry Owen:* Give me the onions.
> *Mrs Cherry Owen:* Ooh, you were drunk as a deacon,
> and sprawling and bawling.
> *Cherry Owen:* Give me a kiss.
> *Mrs Cherry Owen:* And then you sang *Aberystwyth*.
> And then you did a dance on the table.
> *Cherry Owen:* I did?
> *Mrs Cherry Owen:* Drop dead!
> *Cherry Owen:* And then what did I do?
> *Mrs Cherry Owen:* Then you sang *Aberystwyth* all
> over again.   C

D 33, 8–9: ND 37, 4–5
and you said, 'God has come home!' you said,

> 'God has come home!' [*Underlined, with production
> note*] Give it more   N1

D 33, 13: ND 37, 9
Was I wounded?

> [*Production note*] temporary concern   N1

D 33, 16: ND 37, 12
and you said, 'Does anybody want a fight!'

> want a fight?   MS—B2

D 33, 18: ND 37, 15
Give me a kiss.

> [me *altered to*] us   N1 N2

D 33, 20: ND 37, 17–18
And then you sang 'Bread of Heaven', tenor and bass.

> And then you sang [1] Aberystwyth, tenor and bass.
>   MS—A

---

[1] *See p. 47.*

79

D 33, 22: ND 37, 20
I *always* sing 'Bread of Heaven'
   I always sing Aberystwyth.   MS—A

D 34, 15–16: ND 38, 17–18
and you snored all night like a brewery.
   and you [snored *deleted*] breathed [*inserted*] all night
                               N1
   [*End of fair copy written in D.T.'s hand. Remainder of*
   script is mainly the typescript used for C, with manu-
   script corrections and interpolations in D.T.'s hand:
   this typescript starts with the lines] And then you did
   a dance on the table [*to* D 34, 2: ND 38, 4] And then
   what did I do?[*followed by*] Mrs Cherry Owen: Then
   you sang Aberystwyth all over again.
   [*In the margin beside these lines is a vertical line in ink,*
   with the note] rewrite   MS

D 34, 19: ND 38, 21
From Beynon Butchers in Coronation Street,
   [*Text resumes*]   BO M

D 35, 2: ND 39, 7
She ought to do, Bess. It's her brother's.
   She ought to, Bess. It's her brothers [*sic*]   BO
   [sister's *inserted, and then deleted, above*] brother's.
                               N1
D 35, 14: ND 39, 19
It was doctored, mind.
   neutered [*inserted above* doctored, *which is not*
   deleted]   N1
   neutered [*inserted above* doctored, *which is deleted*]
                               N2
   neutered   M
   [*Footnote*] For American audiences: for 'doctored'
   read 'neutered'.   DA

D 35, 15–16: ND 39, 20–21

MRS BEYNON (*Hysterical*) What's that got to do with it?
[*These two lines not in* BO. *Instead*] (*Mrs Beynon Screams*)   BO

D 35, 18: ND 39, 23
Yesterday we had mole.
Yesterday, we had mole.   BO MS—B2 M

D 36, 6–7: ND 40, 15–16
And now I am going out after the corgies, with my little cleaver.
after the corgies with   BO
after corgies, with   C
after the [corgies *deleted*, squirrels *inserted and deleted*] corgies [*restored*]   MS
after the spaniels   M

D 36, 11–12: ND 40, 21–22
Up the street in the Sailors Arms, Sinbad Sailors, grandson of Mary Ann Sailors,
Up the street, in the Sailors' Arms, Ocky Pint, grandson of Mary Ann the Sailors,   BO

D 36, 18: ND 41, 4
SINBAD
[*Ocky Pint   deleted*] Sinbad [*inserted*]   MS

D 36, 24: ND 41, 10
under the dancing underclothes, and left.
the dancing vests,   BO
[vests *deleted*] underclothes [*inserted*]   MS

D 36, 24–37, 4: ND 41, 10–18
A baby cries [*to*] and the children shrilled off to school
[*omitted*]   M

81

D 36, 24: ND 41, 10–11
A baby cries.

    [*Production note*] Nancy cry here   N1
    [*Sound effect of baby crying*]   C A

D 36, 26–27: ND 41, 12–13
OLD MAN: I want my pipe and he wants his bottle.

    my pipe, and   BO
    [*These lines omitted*]   DA

D 37, 3–4: ND 41, 17–18
and the children shrilled off to school

    and the children scuttled off to school (*Children's
    Voices, fading*)   BO
    [(Children's voices) *deleted*] *Childrens* [*sic*] *voices up
    & out*   MS
    Children's voices up and out   B1—B2

D 37, 5: ND 41, 19
SECOND VOICE

    [*1st Voice deleted*] *2nd Voice* [*inserted*]   MS

D 37, 7–8: ND 41, 21–22
drifts slowly in the dab-filled bay, and, lying on his back

    bay, lying on his back   BO C
    bay, and [*inserted*] lying on his back   MS

D 37, 9–10: ND 41, 23–24
among crabs' legs and tangled lines, looks up at the
spring sky.

    lines, [and *inserted and deleted*] looks up   MS

D 37, 19: ND 42, 7
Mr Edwards, in butterfly-collar and straw hat

    in Sunday butterfly-collar   BO
    Mr Mog Edwards   C

D 37, 20–22: ND 42, 8–10
measures with his eye the dawdlers-by for striped flannel
shirts and shrouds and flowery blouses,
    measures, with his eye, the dawdlers by, for
                                        BO MS—B2 M
    striped flannel shirts and flowery blouses   BO

D 37, 22–23: ND 42, 10–11
and bellows to himself in the darkness behind his eye
    to himself, in   BO MS—B2 M

D 37, 25: ND 42, 13
I love Miss Price.
    I love Miss Myfanwy Price.   BO

D 38, 2: ND 42, 17
like short silver policemen.
    like short, silver policemen   BO MS—B2 M

D 38, 6–7: ND 42, 21–22
School bell in background. Children's voices. The noise of
children's feet on the cobbles
    [*After sound of school bell*] *1st Voice:* He hears the
    voices of children, and the noise of children's feet on
    the cobbles   C
    [*School bell in background Childrens* typescript
    deleted in ink: marked STET *in ink. 1st Voice* He hears
    the [*inserted in pencil, deleted in ink*] voices [of
    children *inserted and deleted in ink*] *The noise of*
    children's feet on the cobbles   MS
    [*School bell in background. Children's voices deleted*]
    He hears the voices of children and [*inserted*] the
    noise of children's feet on the cobbles   N1

D 38, 9–10: ND 42, 24–25
Ricky Rhys, Tommy Powell, our Sal, little Gerwain,
Billy Swansea
    Ricky Rhys, our Sal, Billy Swansea   PA

D 38, 18: ND 43, 4
A burst of yelping crying
> [*Sound of Billy yelping and Maggie crying*]   C

D 38, 19: ND 43, 5
It's Billy.
> That's Billy.   BO C MS
> It's Billy. [*Typing error in* B1, *not corrected*]

D 38, 21: ND 43, 7   N1 N2 B2
And the children's voices cry away.
> (The Children's Voices and Noises Fade)   BO
> a [(*The children's voices and noises fade*
> b *Out, school bell*
> c *Clip-clop of horses feet on cobbles*)
> d *Captain Cat:* (*loudly*) Morning, Big Ben.
> e *Man's Voice:* Morning, Captain.
> f (*Clip-clop fades*)
> g (*Noise of child running on cobbles*)
> h *Captain Cat:* (*softly to himself*) Glyndur [*sic*]
>   Jones,
> i late again. (*Loudly*) You'll cop it, Glyndur. Put
> j a book down your breeches.
> k (*Noise of child on cobbles fades*)
> l (*Postman's rat-tat on door, distant*)
>
> *Lines a–l in typescript*
> *Lines f and g deleted in pencil: narration inserted*
> *in pencil* (*for stage reading*):
>
> *1st Voice:* Captan [*sic*] Cat hears one last child
> running to school.
> *Complete passage deleted in ink*]
> *1st Voice:* And the children's voices cry away
> [*inserted in ink*]   MS

D 38, 22: ND 43, 8
Postman's rat-a-tat on door, distant
> [*Postman's rat-tat on door, distant   deleted in pencil*]
>   MS
> *Postman's rat-a-tat on door. Distant.* [*inserted*] N1 N2

84

D 38, 22–42, 7: ND 43, 8–47, 2
Postman's rat-a-tat [*to*] Pint of Stout. And no egg in.
[*Not in*]   BO

D 39, 23: ND 44, 11
And come home at all hours covered with feathers.
[*Production note*] No question   N1

D 39, 24: ND 44, 12
I don't want persons in my nice clean rooms
   my *nice clean* rooms   MS—B2 M ND
   my nice clean rooms   D DA

D 40, 8: ND 44, 24–25
And back she goes to the kitchen to polish the potatoes.
   to the kitchen, to polish   MS—B2

D 40, 10–16: ND 45, 1–5
FIRST VOICE   Captain Cat hears Willy Nilly's feet heavy
on the distant cobbles.
CAPTAIN CAT   One, two, three, four, five . . . That's Mrs
Rose Cottage.
  [(*Noise of slow, heavy feet on cobbles, distant*) *deleted*]
   1st V. Captain cat hears Willy Nilly's feet heavy on
   the distant cobbles. [*inserted in pencil*]
   Captain Cat: One, two, three, four, five. . . . . . .
   [*eight full points*] [(*rat-a-tat. Still distant*) *Typescript*
   deleted in ink]
   Captain Cat: That's Mrs Rose Cottage.   MS
   [*1st Voice: omitted through typing error*] Here's
   Willy Nilly's feet heavy on the distant cobbles . . .
   One, two, three, four, five . . .   B1
   [Here's *deleted*] *1st Voice:* Captain Cat hears
   [*inserted*] Willy Nilly's feet heavy on the distant
   cobbles . . . *Capt. Cat:* [*inserted*] One, two, three, four,
   five . . .   N1 N2

85

D 40, 16–17: ND 45, 7–8

from her sister in Gorslas. How's the twins' teeth?
He's stopping at School House.

in Gors-glas. [*sic throughout*]   C—M
from her sister in Gors-glas. How's the twins' teeth?
[(*Noise of feet on cobbles   typescript deleted: 1st*
Voice: The postman's *insertion in ink deleted*]
coming nearer) [*typescript not deleted.*]
[*Captain Cat:* six, seven, eight. Plain sealed brown
envelope [1] from Liverpool for the lodger in Craig-y-
don. Don't stick a pin in it, Willy.
Captain Cat: nine, ten, eleven, twelve, thirteen.
Entire passage deleted in pencil.]
[(*Rat-a-tat. Closer*) *deleted in ink*]
Captain Cat: He's stopping at School House.   MS
Plain sealed brown envelope from Liverpool for the
lodger in Craig-y-don. Don't stick a pin in it, Willy
. . . nine, ten, eleven, twelve, thirteen (*knocking*)
Captain Cat: He's stopping at School House.   C

D 41, 2: ND 45, 21

A book called *Lives of the Great Poisoners.*
A book called *Lives of the Great Poisoners.*
[(*Door slams*)
(*Feet on cobbles*)
(*Shop bell rings*)   *typescript deleted*]   MS

---

1 *The significance of a plain sealed brown envelope for
the mailing of contraceptives may have been lost on the
American audience at the New York reading on May 14,
1953; for no audience reaction is recorded in* C (*the
Caedmon L.P.*). *This may have led to the deletion of the
passage. Alternatively, of course, it may have been cut
because blind Captain Cat could not see the envelope; but
the sentence could have been transferred to Willy Nilly,
who, in another deleted passage (D 41, 9: ND 46, 2),
animadverts upon the lodger's behaviour.*

D 41, 8–9: ND 46, 1–2
Mr Pugh's bought a book now on how to do in Mrs Pugh.
    [*Production note*] slower   N1
    how to do in Mrs Pugh, and there's careful the
    lodger is getting in Craig-y-don.   c
    [and there's careful the lodger is getting in Craig-y-
    don . . . *deleted in pencil*]   MS

D 41, 13–19: ND 46, 6–12
Smelling of lavender today [*to*] twenty-one X's.
    [*Omitted*]   M

D 41, 23–42, 7: ND 46, 16–47, 2
Slow feet on cobbles [*to*] And no egg in.
    [*Omitted*]   M

D 41, 23: ND 46, 16:
Slow feet on cobbles, quicker feet approaching
    [*Sound effect omitted*]
    1st Voice: Down the street comes Willy Nilly, and
    Captain Cat hears other steps approaching.   c
    [*Sound effect deleted in pencil:*
    1st V. Down the street comes Willy Nilly & Captain
    Cat hears other steps approaching *inserted in pencil*
    and then deleted in ink; sound effect then restored with
    stet *in ink*]   MS
    [*Sound effect deleted*] *1st Voice:* Down the street
    comes Willy Nilly, and Captain Cat hears other
    steps approaching [*inserted*]   N1

D 41, 25–26: ND 46, 18–20
Pint of stout with a egg in it. *Footsteps stop*
    an egg   c—B2
    [(*Footsteps stop*) *Typescript deleted in pencil*]   MS
    [*Footsteps stop not in*]   B1 N1 N2

D 42, 3–5: ND 46, 24–26
FIRST VOICE The quick footsteps hurry on along the
cobbles and up three steps to the Sailors Arms.
    1st Voice: [*inserted in pencil:* (*bracket deleted*] *The*

quick footsteps hurry on along the cobbles and up
three steps [typescript of sound effect turned into
narration   ) bracket deleted] to the Sailors Arms
[inserted in pencil]   MS
and up [three steps *deleted*] the steps *[inserted]* N1 N2
[Entire passage omitted]   DA

D 42, 9–10: ND 47, 4–5
People are moving now up and down the cobbled street,
    a [(*Fade out*)
    b (*Fade in*)
    c (*Noise of people, moving up and down the cobbled*
       street)
    d (*Indistinguishable murmur of voices passing*)
Lines a, b, d, and first two words of c deleted in
pencil: *1st V. inserted in pencil before* people: are
before moving: now *before* up: *finally, entire passage
deleted in ink, and fair copy, as in* D *and in* ND,
written out again in pencil]   MS
(*Now the Noise of Many Feet on the Cobbles, and an
Indistinguishable Murmur of Voices*)   BO

D 42, 12–43, 6: ND 47, 7–48, 2
All the women are out [*to*] Organ Morgan's at it early.
    Mrs Cadwalladwr going to the butchers. Mr Nappo
and Evan Davies talking fish. Can't hear what the
women are gossipping round the pump. Same as
ever. Who's having a baby, who blacked whose eye,
seen Mrs Phillips' new mauve jumper, it's her old
one dyed, who's dead, who's dying, the cost of
soapflakes
(*Children's Voices Chanting in Background*)
Captain Cat: One, Two,
          Buckle my shoe,
          Three, four,
          Knock at my door,
          Five, six,
          Chopping up sticks,
88

> Six, seven,
> Going to heaven . . .
> (*Chapel Organ in Distance*)
> *Captain Cat:* Organ Morgan's at it early . . .   BO
> [*End of version, unfinished, in Botteghe Oscure, with
> footnote*] (to be continued)   BO

D 42, 13: ND 47, 8
You can tell it's Spring.
> You can tell it's spring.   M

D 42, 13–14: ND 47, 8–9
you can tell her by her trotters,
> by her hooves,   C
> her [hooves *deleted*] trotters [*inserted*]   MS
> [*Note on* her trotters] not hooves   N1

D 42, 16: ND 47, 10–11
What can you talk about flatfish?
> Now what can you talk about flatfish?   C

D 42, 20: ND 47, 14
her pet black cat, it follows her everywhere,
> her pet black cat, follows her everywhere   C

D 42, 24: ND 47, 17
Mrs Rose Cottage's eldest Mae,
> Mrs Rose Cottage's eldest, Mae,   MS—B2 M

D 42, 28: ND 47, 21–22
Can't hear what the women are gabbing round the pump.
> gabbing [*underlined in pencil: may not imply italic*]
>   MS
> gabbing [*not corrected in* N1]   B1 N1 N2

D 43, 1–2: ND 47, 25–26
seen Mrs Beynon's new mauve jumper, it's her old grey
jumper dyed,
> mauve jumper it's her old grey   MS

89

D 43, 6: ND 48, 2
You can tell it's Spring.
    You can *tell* it's *Spring*. [*underlined in pencil*]   MS
    You can *tell* it's *Spring*.   B1
    [*Underlining of Spring deleted*]   N1 N2
    You can *tell* it's Spring.   M ND
    [*After* You can *tell* it's *Spring*.
    (*Children's voices chanting, distant*)
    Captain Cat (*softly, in time with the singing*)
    [*space for line of song?*]
    (*the Children's voices fade*)
    (*Organ Morgan is still heard in background*)
    (*Noise of milk cans*)
    This passage deleted in ink]   MS

D 43, 7–8: ND 48, 4–5
FIRST VOICE And he hears the noise of milk-cans.
    [*Inserted in place of* (*noise of milk-cans*) *deleted*]
                                           MS
    [*Omitted*]   DA

D 43, 11–12: ND 48, 8–9
Snuffle on, Ocky, watering the town . . . Somebody's
coming.
    Snuffle on, Ocky, watering the town.
    [*Up indistinguishable murmur of voices typescript
    deleted in pencil*]
    Somebody's coming.   MS

D 43, 13: ND 48, 10–11
Now the voices round the pump can see somebody
coming.
    can see somebody's coming.   C

D 43, 20–21: ND 48, 17–18
Hullo, Polly my love, can you hear the dumb goose-hiss
of the wives
    Hullo, Polly, my love,
    2nd Voice: can you hear   C MS

Hullo, Polly, my love,
2nd Voice [inserted] Can [c *altered to* C]   N1 N2

D 43, 27–28: ND 48, 24–25
you're one mother won't wriggle her roly poly bum or pat
her fat little buttery feet
    [won't wriggle her roly poly bum or [1] *omitted*]   A
    little buttery foot   C—A

D 44, 3: ND 48, 29
A cock crows
    [*No sound effect*] *1st Voice:* A cock crows.   C
    [*Sound effect deleted. 1st Voice* A cock crows
    inserted and deleted in ink]
    [*Production note*] Louder [*perhaps implying that a*
    reader crowed aloud] *A cock crows* [*inserted in ink,*
    restoring sound effect for radio]   MS
    1st Voice: (*if necc.*) [*inserted before*] *A cock crows* N1
    Organ music out [*inserted on separate line before*] *A*
    cock crows.   M

D 44, 6: ND 49, 3
SECOND VOICE
    1st Voice   C
    [*1st deleted*] *2nd* [*inserted*]   MS

D 44, 9: ND 49, 6
Organ music fades into silence
    Out background organ music [*sound effect in type-*
    script deleted in pencil; restored in ink]   MS
    Out background organ music   B1
    Out background organ music [*transferred to* D 44, 3:
    ND 48, 29]   N1 N2 B2

---

[1] *See p. 43.*

D 44, 10: ND 49, 7
FIRST VOICE
    Captain Cat: C
    [*Captain Cat: deleted*] *1st* Voice [*inserted*]   MS
    [*1st Voice: deleted: Capt. Cat inserted and deleted*]
    1st Voice [*restored*]   N1

D 44, 20: ND 49, 17
scamper of sanderlings,
    [sand *written above* sander *and then deleted: possibly*
    sandlings *was considered*]   MS

D 44, 22: ND 49, 19–20
the ragged gabble of the beargarden school
    of the slovenly beargarden school   C
    [slovenly *deleted*]   MS

D 44, 25: ND 49, 22
rat-traps, shrimp-nets,
    rat-traps, senna pods, shrimp nets   C
    [senna pods *deleted*]   MS

D 44, 27: ND 49, 24
FIRST WOMAN
    [*Sequence to* D 47, 4: ND 52, 12 *played by two*
    women only]   C
    [*Woman altered to Neighbour throughout se-*
    quence]   B2 C

D 45, 7: ND 50, 7
THIRD WOMAN
    [*4th deleted*] *3rd* [*inserted*]   MS
    [*ditto in* D 45, 12, 18, 21, D 46, 7, 17, 23, D 47, 3:
    ND 50, 12, 18, ND 51, 1, 12, 22, ND 52, 5, 11]   MS

D 45, 17: ND 50, 17
even though he hanged his collie.
    [killed his collie *deleted*: hanged *inserted and deleted*:
    even though he hanged his collie *rewritten*]   MS
92

D 45, 18–27: ND 50, 18–51, 4
THIRD WOMAN [*to*] pull it off and eat it.
   [*Deleted*]   N1 N2
   [*Omitted*]   M
   pull it off and eat it—   MS B1 B2

D 45, 23: ND 50, 23
go on, he's pulling her leg
   Go on he's pulling her leg   B1 B2

D 46, 1, 21: ND 51, 5, 52, 4
FOURTH WOMAN
   [*5th deleted*] *4th* [*inserted in pencil*]   MS

D 46, 4: ND 51, 9
Look at that Nogood Boyo now
   no-good Boyo   MS B1 B2
   [no-good *altered to* Nogood: *sic throughout*] N1 N2

D 46, 24: ND 52, 6
And how's Organ Morgan, Mrs Morgan?
   Mrs Morgan [*no question-mark*]   MS—N2 M

D 47, 9–14: ND 52, 17–22
It runs through the hedges [*to*] springing in the young sun.
   [*Omitted*]   M

D 47, 15–19: ND 52, 23–53, 2
SECOND VOICE [*to*] Lie down.
   [*Transferred to follow* D 47, 25: ND 53, 8)   DA

D 47, 16–17: ND 52, 24–25
Evans the Death presses hard with black gloves on the coffin of his breast
   Thomas the Death   C MS B1
   [Thomas *deleted*] Evans [*inserted*: *ditto in* D 47, 18: ND 53, 1]   N1 N2
   presses hard, with black gloves, on the coffin of his breast,   MS—B2 M

D 47, 21: ND 53, 4
Gossamer Beynon
    [Rosemary *deleted*] Gossamer [*inserted: ditto in*
    D 47, 23: ND 53, 6]   MS

D 47, 26–48, 3: ND 53, 9–16
SECOND VOICE [*to*] the foot that belongs to this shoe.
    [*Omitted*]   DA

D 47, 27: ND 53, 10
Spring this strong morning foams in a flame
    flame [*typescript underlined in ink*]   MS
    flame   B1
    [*underlining of* flame *deleted*]   N1 N2

D 48, 8–9: ND 53, 21–22
No, *I'll* take the mulatto, by God, who's captain here?
Parlez-vous jig jig, Madam?
    who's captain here.   MS—N2 M
    [Parlez-vous jig jig, Madam? *omitted*]   M

D 48, 17–18: ND 54, 4–5
A choir of children's voices suddenly cries out
    [*Sound effect omitted*]   A DA

D 48, 23: ND 54, 10
Mr Mog Edwards' letter
    Mr Mog Edwards's letter   C MS

D 48, 27–28: ND 54, 14–15
hens at the back door whimper and snivel for the lickerish
bog-black tea.
    for their lickerish   C

D 49, 2–3: ND 54, 18
Sole Prop: Mr Mog Edwards (late of Twll),
    (late of Brynhyfryd),   C
                            94

[(late of Twill ¹) *typescript deleted*]
(late of Twll) [*inserted in ink*]   MS

D 49, 15–17: ND 54, 30–55, 2
A new parcel of ribbons has come from Carmarthen today, all the colours of the rainbow.
> from Carmarthen today [today *inserted in pencil: no comma*] all the colours   MS

D 49, 22–24: ND 55, 7–9
He is a proper Christian. Not like Cherry Owen who said you should have thrown her back he said. Business is very poorly.
> Not like Butcher Beynon who said you should have thrown her back he said. [This was in the dream *deleted*] Business is very poorly.   MS

D 49, 25–27: ND 55, 10–12
she never got stockings so what is the use I say. Mr Waldo tried to sell me a woman's nightie outsize
> what is the use I say. Butcher Beynon bought a check cap to go badgering he said. Mr Waldo tried   c
> [Butcher Beynon bought a check cap to go badgering he said *typescript deleted in pencil: note in margin in pencil* Out *deleted in ink*]   MS
> [*Note in margin*] Cut—the Butcher Beynon line ²   N1

---

¹ *'Twill' was evidently a valiant attempt on the part of the American typist to make something pronounceable out of 'Twll', the Welsh word for 'arse-hole': which gives point to the name of the local newspaper, the* Twll Bugle (D 49, 11: ND 54, 26).

² *Presumably this means that D.T. noticed that the Butcher Beynon line had been cut in* B1 (*the B.B.C. duplicated script supplied to him when* MS *was lost*); *he may have forgotten that he himself cut it in* MS.

95

D 49, 28–29: ND 55, 13–14
I sold a packet of pins to Tom the Sailors to pick his
teeth.
    [*Thus in all versions*] [1]   C—DA

D 49, 29: ND 55, 14–15
If this goes on I shall be in the workhouse.
    in the poorhouse   C B1—M ND
    [Work *deleted in pencil*] Poor [*inserted in pencil*]
    house.   MS
    [*Footnote*] For American audiences: for 'workhouse'
    read 'poorhouse'.   DA

D 50, 1: ND 55, 17–18
in His Heavenly Mansion.
    in [this *deleted*: his *deleted*] His [*inserted in pencil*] MS

D 50, 9–10: ND 55, 26–27
and sees, in sudden Springshine,
    in sudden Spring sunshine, [*typing error*]   B1
    [B1 *not corrected*]   N1 N2 A M
    [*Correct version*] Springshine,   C MS B2
    in sudden Springshine, [(*seabirds and soft sea noise*)
    typescript deleted in pencil]   MS

D 50, 14: ND 56, 1
the fishy sea smooth to the sea's end as it lulls in blue.
    [*Production note in pencil, deleted in ink*] Lazier MS

D 50, 19–20: ND 56, 6–7
the fishermen gaze at that milkmaid whispering water
    milk-mild   C M
    milk-maid [*typing error?*]   MS
    milk-maid   B1 N2 A
    milk- [*maid altered by D.T. to*] mild   N1

---

[1] *It must have been by an oversight that D.T. did not
alter the name to Sinbad.*

D 50, 24: ND 56, 11
Too rough for fishing today.
>Too rough for fishing today. [—Lazier *production
note in pencil, deleted in ink*]   MS

D 50, 3–4: ND 56, 20–22
Captain Cat at his window says soft to himself the words
of their song.
>[(*Children singing* [1] *in background*) *typescript deleted
in pencil*]   MS

D 51, 21: ND 57, 10
Long pause
>[(*The children's singing fades*) *typescript deleted in
pencil*] *Long pause* [*inserted in pencil*]   MS
>[Long *deleted*] A [*inserted*] pause.   N1 N2
>A pause   M

D 51, 24: ND 57, 13
It is 'the Rustle of Spring'.
>That music is [*may be impromptu alteration after
audience laughter*]   C
>(*singing of glee-party in counterpoint with children*)
>   DA

D 52, 2: ND 57, 20
and dogs bark blue in the face.
>And the dogs   C B1—B2 A M
>And [the *deleted*] dogs   MS
>The morning is all singing [*transferred from* D53, 24:
ND 59, 22]
>(*Glee party and children reach final chord*)
>*End of Act One*   DA

---

[1] *The song 'Johnnie Crack' and Polly Garter's song*
(D 59, 66: ND 60, 73) *are also printed in* SELECTED LETTERS
OF DYLAN THOMAS, 1966: *Letter to Theodore Roethke,
June 15, 1953.*

D 52, 3–7: ND 57, 22–25
Mrs Ogmore Pritchard belches [*to*] from one of the fingerbowls, a primrose grows.

[*Omitted*]	DA
a primrose grows [*typescript underlined in ink*]	MS
a primrose grows	B1 N1 N2 M
[(*Now the children's voices are heard again in the background, singing another tune, softly and word-lessly*) *typescript deleted in pencil*]	MS
Act Two	
(*Children's song* [*Johnnie Crack*] *and glee song heard together. On last line of singing: Curtain Up*)	DA

D 52, 11: ND 58, 4
one darkly one plumply blooming in the quick, dewy sun.

in the quicky, dewy sun.	C
quick [y *deleted in ink*]	MS

D 52, 13–14: ND 58, 6–7
in the lap of her dirty yellow petticoat, hard against her hard dark thighs.

[yellow *deleted*] scarlet [*inserted*]	N1 N2
scarlet	M
her dark thighs [hard *omitted in error*]	DA

D 52, 16: ND 58, 9–10
Cross my palm with silver. Out of our housekeeping money.

Out of the housekeeping money.	C
[the *deleted*] our [*inserted*]	MS

D 52, 24: ND 58, 17
God is Love, the text says.

God is love, the text says.	MS—B2 M

D 52, 26: ND 58, 19
That's *our* bed.

[*Production note in pencil*]!!!!!!	MS

D 53, 2: ND 58, 25
It's Dai, it's Dai Bread!
    [*Production note in pencil*]!!!!!   MS

D 53, 4: ND 59, 2
The featherbed's floating back.
    The bed's floating back.   C

D 53, 22: ND 59, 20
Pause. The children's singing fades
    (*Chord of children's voices*)   C
    [*Sound effect deleted*]   N1 N2

D 53, 24: ND 59, 22
The morning is all singing.
    [Transferred to D 52, 2: ND 57, 20]   DA

D 53, 24–27: ND 59, 22–25
The Reverend Eli Jenkins, [*to*] the Mothers' Union Dance
tonight.
    [*Transferred to follow* D 54, 13: ND 60, 13]   DA

D 54, 9: ND 60, 9
little Willy Wee and he's six feet deep.
    deep [*No full point here or in lines* 13, 21 *or* 25]   MS

D 54, 11: ND 60, 11
And I'll never have such loving again.
    [*Production note in margin*] Lov*ing* not lovin'   N1

D 54, 13: ND 54, 13
Little Willy Wee was the man for me
    [Wee was *deleted*] Weaẑel is [*inserted with* s *above* z
    as alternative spelling]   N1
    [Wee *deleted*] Weazel   N2
    Weasel   M
    The Reverend Eli Jenkins, [*to*] the Mothers' Union
    Dance tonight. [*Inserted from* D 53, 24–27: ND 59,
    22–25]   DA

D 54, 14–25: ND 60, 14–25
Now men from every parish round [*to*] Little Willy
Weazel is the man for me.
[*Omitted*]   M

D 54, 25: ND 60, 25
Little Willy Weazel is the man for me.
[Was *deleted*] is [*inserted*]   MS
Was [*Letter to Theodore Roethke, June 15, 1953*]

D 54, 29–30: ND 61, 2–3
And the Reverend Jenkins hurries on through the town to
visit the sick with jelly and poems.
    on through the town, to visit the sick   MS

D 55, 1: ND 61, 5
FIRST VOICE
    2nd Voice   C
    [2nd *deleted*] 1st [*inserted*]   MS

D 55, 13–56, 12: ND 61, 16–62, 22
SINBAD   Oh, Mr Waldo, [*to*] POLLY GARTER again.
    [*Omitted*]   M

D 55, 18–19: ND 61, 21–22
I dote on that Gossamer Beynon. She's a lady all over.
    I dote on that Gossamer Beynon.
    a   *2nd Voice:* Love, sings the Spring. The bedspring
    b   grass bounces under birds' bums and lambs.
    c   *1st Voice:* And Gossamer Beynon, schoolteacher,
    d   spoonstirred and quivering, teaches her slubber-
         degullion class
    e   *Children's Voices:* It was a luvver and his lars
    f   With a a and a o and a a nonino . . .
    g   *Gossamer Beynon:* Naow, naow, naow, your
         eccents, children!
    h   It was a lover and his less
    j   With a hey and a hao and a hey nonino . . .
    k   *Sinbad:* Oh, Mr Waldo,
100

1 *1st Voice:* says Sinbad Sailors,
  Sinbad: she's a lady all over.   c
[*Text a–l identical with* c *in typescript faintly deleted
by two pencil-strokes: with notes in pencil at bottom
of page 33 of* MS.   For Tenby out *and at top of page
34* Out for Tenby *both deleted in ink*]   MS
[*Text identical with* c][1]   N1 N2 B2
[*Text of* c *in Footnote*]   DA

D 55, 18*a*: ND 61, 21*a*
Love, sings the Spring.
[*Production note*] more singing   MS

D 55, 18*b*: ND 61, 21*b*
[*Production note* No *the* *deleted*]   N1

D 55, 18*k*: ND 61, 21*k*
Sinbad: Oh, Mr Waldo
[*Production note*] more   N1

D 55, 27–56, 12: ND 62, 8–22
And if only grandma'd *die*, [*to*] again.
  [*Deleted in pencil, with note in pencil* Out for Tenby
  deleted in ink. Note in ink] Stet   MS

D 56, 2–3: ND 62, 12–13
When birds do sing hey ding a ding a ding
Sweet lovers love the Spring . . .
  When birds do sing a ding a ding a ding
  Sweet Luvvers luv the Spring . . .   MS—B2

---

[1] *As this passage, deleted with the note 'Out for Tenby',
had not been marked 'Stet', it was not typed in* B1, *of
which copies were given to Dylan Thomas before he left for
New York. The passage was accordingly typed in New
York, presumably dictated by Dylan Thomas from memory,
and typescript copies were inserted in* N1 *and* N2.

D 57, 2–18: ND 63, 15–64, 5
Kiss me in Goosegog Lane [*to*] Go on, Gwennie.
[*Omitted*]   M

D 57, 23: ND 63, 10
SECOND BOY
  First Boy: M

D 58, 1: ND 63, 15
SECOND BOY
  1st Boy: M

D 58, 11: ND 65, 4
Kiss me in Milk Wood Dicky
  [*Note in pencil*] a bird in a bush   MS

D 58, 15, 20, 59, 1, 8: ND 65, 1, 6, 13, 20
THIRD BOY
  2nd Boy: M

D 59, 26: ND 66, 14
the loose wild barefoot women
  the loose wild barefoot knickerless women   MS

D 59, 28: ND 66, 16
for her cawl and buttermilk
  her cowl [1]   MS—B2 M

D 60, 3–14: ND 66, 20–31
Then his tormentors tussle [*to*] pop goes the weasel and
the wind.
  [*Omitted*]   M

D 60, 7–10: ND 66, 24–27
gobstoppers big as wens that rainbow as you suck, [*to*]
nougat to tug and ribbon out
  gobstoppers big as wens that rainbow as you suck,

---

[1] *The Welsh 'cawl', a broth of mutton, leeks and
potatoes, is pronounced 'cowl'.*

humbugs, winegums, a hot pennorth of brandyballs,
hundreds and thousands, liquorice sweet as sick,
tooth-loosening toffee of tar, nugget to tug and
ribbon out   C
    gobstoppers big as wens that rainbow as you suck,
[humbugs *deleted*] brandyballs [*inserted*], winegums
[a hot pennorth of brandyballs *deleted*], hundreds
and thousands, liquorice sweet as sick, [tooth-
loosening toffee of tar, *deleted*] nugget to tug and
ribbon out [cut *added in margin and deleted*] cut
[*re-inserted: probably for Tenby*]   MS

D 60, 11–12: ND 66, 28–29
crimson coughdrops to spit blood, ice-cream cornets,
    crimson coughdrops to spit blood, stale bags of
    black boiled marbles, ice-cream cornets,   C
    crimson coughdrops to spit blood, [stale bags of
    black boiled marbles, *deleted*] ice-cream cornets, MS

D 60, 13–14: ND 66, 30–31
pop goes the weasel and the wind.
    the weazel and the wind.   MS—B2

D 60, 15: ND 67, 1
SECOND VOICE
    1st Voice [*i.e. Dylan Thomas*]   C
    [*2nd deleted in pencil: 1st inserted in pencil and
    deleted in ink*] *2nd* [*restored in ink*]   MS
    [*Note in pencil* (*not in D.T.'s hand*): Perhaps Dylan
    take these lines too: *deleted in pencil*]   MS

D 60, 20–21: ND 67, 6–7
Eyes run from the trees and windows of the street,
steaming 'Gossamer',
    of the street steaming,[1] 'Gossamer',   MS—B2 M

---

[1] *Probably an error in punctuation. There is nothing in
the Caedmon recording,* C, *to suggest that the comma
signifies a pause.*

D 60, 24–26: ND 67, 10–12
Sinbad Sailors places on her thighs still dewdamp from
the first mangrowing cockcrow garden his reverent, goat-
bearded hands.
>Sinbad Sailors places on her his reverent goat-
>bearded hands.   M

D 61, 4–5: ND 67, 21–22
she tells the stripped and mother-of-the-world big-
beamed and Eve-hipped spring of her self.
>[*Production note*] More   MS

D 61, 8: ND 67, 24
so long as he's all cucumber and hooves
>so long as he's all hooves.   M
>*cucumber* [*underlined, with production note*] first word
>stronger   N1

D 61, 18: ND 68, 7
He grieves to his guinness,
>guiness.   MS—N2
>Guiness.   M
>Guinness,   ND

D 61, 20–22: ND 68, 9–11
Oh, beautiful beautiful Gossamer B., I wish I wish that
you were for me. I wish you were not so educated.
>that you were for me. Why are you so educated?   C
>I wish I wish that you were for me [*added in pencil*
>*above typescript*]   MS
>[I wish you were not *deleted*] Why are you [*inserted*]
>so educated [. *altered to* ? *which is then deleted*] .
>[*restored*]   N1
>Why are you so educated [*Production note in* N3 *only*]
>angry   N3

D 61, 24–28: ND 68, 13–17
She feels his goatbeard tickle her [*to*] and the kidneys of
lambs.
>[*Deleted in pencil with note* Not for Tenby *in pencil,*
>*deleted in ink. Note added in ink*] Stet   MS

D 61, 25-27: ND 68, 14-16
and she turns in a terror of delight away from his whips
and whiskery conflagration, and sits down in the kitchen
   turns, in a terror of delight, away from   MS—B2 M
   conflagration and sits down   MS—B2 M

D 62, 6-7: ND 68, 23-24
He has bound a plain brown-paper cover round the book.
   over the book.   C

D 63, 6-7: ND 69, 22-24
a venomous porridge unknown to toxicologists which
will scald and viper through her
   toxologists   C—N2 M
   scald and [serpent *deleted*] viper [*inserted in ink*]   MS

D 63, 13-14: ND 70, 6-7
and quick as a flash he ducks her in rat soup.
   quick as a [flywhisk *deleted*] flash [*inserted in ink*]   MS

D 63, 25-26: ND 70, 18-19
She was martyred again last night. Mrs Organ Morgan
saw her with Mr Waldo.
   last night [in Milk Wood *deleted*] . [*inserted*] cut [*or*]
   out [*in pencil in margin, later deleted in ink: possibly*
   signifying Out for Tenby] [*note in D.C.'s hand* stet in
   Milk Wood *later deleted*]   MS
   last night [, *deleted*] in Milk Wood   N1 N2 M
   with Mr Waldo in Milk Wood.   DA

D 64, 7-8: ND 71, 4-5
Oh, they didn't fool me.
   [*Production note*] More   MS

D 64, 16: ND 71, 13
a woman that can't say No even to midgets
   midgets [*typescript underlined in ink*]   MS

D 64, 17: ND 71, 14
Remember Bob Spit?
    Remember Tom Spit?   C M DA
    Remember [Tom *deleted*] Bob [*inserted in pencil*]
    Spit?   MS
    Remember [Bob *deleted*] Tom [*inserted*] Spit?
                                     N1 N2

D 64, 14–20: ND 71, 16–17
Fred Spit and Arthur. Sometimes I like Fred best
    Dai [*instead of Fred*]   C M
    [Dai *deleted*] Fred [*inserted in ink*]   MS
    Dai [*written above*] Fred [*but neither deleted*]   N1
    [Fred *deleted*] Dai [*inserted*]   N2

D 64, 23–24: ND 71, 20–21
Oh, Bach without any doubt. Bach every time for me.
    Bach [*each time underlined in ink*]   MS
    Oh, *Bach* [*Production note*] more   MS

D 65, 1: ND 71, 25
FIRST VOICE
    [*1st deleted*] *2nd* [*inserted*]   N1

D 65, 7: ND 72, 3
SECOND VOICE
    [*1st deleted in pencil*] 2nd [*inserted in pencil*: *with
    production note, not in D.T.'s hand*] Roy [1] take this!

D 65, 11–12: ND 72, 7–8
a dogdish, marked Fido, of peppery fish-scraps
    peppery salt scraps   C

D 65, 12–14: ND 72, 8–10
and listens to the voices of his sixty-six clocks, one for
each year of his loony age, and watches, with love,
    his sixty-six clocks—(one for each year of his loony
    age)—and watches,   MS—B2 M

---

[1] *Presumably Roy Poole, one of the New York cast.*

D 65, 15–23: ND 72, 11–20
their black-and-white moony loudlipped faces tocking the
earth away: slow clocks, quick clocks, [*to*] clocks with no
hands for ever drumming out time
    tocking the earth away:
    Lord Cut-Glass slow clocks, quick clocks [*to*] clocks
    with no hands
    Narrator: for ever drumming out time   DA

D 65, 30: ND 72, 26
ping, strike, tick, chime, and tock.
    ping, strike, tick chime and tock.   MS—B2 M

D 66, 2–3: ND 72, 28–29
The lust and lilt and lather and emerald breeze and
crackle of the bird-praise and body of Spring
    crackle of the bird-praise, and the body of Spring C

D 66, 12: ND 73, 9
And I'll never have such loving again,
    [*Production note*] casually [1]   MS

D 66, 22: ND 73, 19
A silence
    A long [*inserted*] *silence*   N1 N2 M
    [*Note in* N3 *only*] *Could* be end of Act 1   N3

D 67, 2: ND 73, 27
Pigs grunt in a wet wallow-bath,
    A pride of pigs grunts   C
    [No! *inserted in ink and deleted.* A pride of pigs
    deleted] Pigs [*inserted*] grunts [*sic*]   MS

D 67, 11–68, 9: ND 74, 9–75, 8
MRS PUGH [*to*] he murmurs with a wheedle.
    [*Omitted*]   M

---

[1] *Above 'casually' is written a word that looks like
'parenthis': possibly for 'parenthesis', implying that the
line is to be sung casually, as though in a parenthesis.*

107

D 67, 16: ND 74, 14
do not nod at table.
   do not *nod* at table.   MS—B2

D 67, 17: ND 74, 15
FIRST VOICE
   [*1st deleted*] 2nd [*inserted*]   N1 N2

D 67, 18: ND 74, 16–17
He puts on a soft-soaping smile.
   He [tries to put *altered to*] puts on   MS
   He [*note*] no 'tries' [*above line*] puts on   N1

D 67, 24: ND 74, 22
SECOND VOICE
   First Voice   C

D 68, 1–5: ND 74, 26–75, 4
cauldrons and phials brimful with pox [*to*] a pokerbacked
nutcracker wife.
   [*Production note*] quicker more staccato   N1

D 68, 9: ND 75, 8
he murmurs with a wheedle.
   he murmurs with a wheedle [, and down the coiled
   stairways of her ear seethes boiling hemlock and oil
   deleted].   MS

D 68, 10: ND 75, 9
FIRST VOICE
   2nd Voice   M

D 68, 11–19: ND 75, 10–18
Captain Cat, at his window thrown wide to the sun [*to*]
He weeps as he sleeps and sails.
   Captain Cat, at his wide window, slumbers and
   voyages, tattooed and ear-ringed and rolling on the
   old clippered seas, brawls with broken bottles in the
   fug and babel of the dark dock bars, has a herd of

short and good-time-cows in every naughty port, tattooed with Union Jacks and little women who hula shimmy and ripple and I love you Rosie Probert on his belly he roves those dead sea days and the drowned and cut-throat hair-dyed high-breasted schooner-and-harbour-town dead go with him dancing and slashing and making ghosts' love; and the tears run down his grog-blossomed nose.

[Punctuated above as in typescript version in MS]   C

[Typescript Captain Cat, at his wide window, *continuing as in* C *above, but with the following variations:*

tatooed [hair-dyed high-breasted *deleted*] <u>dancing</u> and <u>slashing</u> [*underlined thus*] *The entire typescript passage deleted in ink.*

Followed by a manuscript draft in ink:

Capt. Cat, at his window thrown wide to the sun and the old, clippered seas, slumbers and voyages; ear-ringed and rolling he brawls with broken bottles in the fug and babel of the dark dock bars; flags and snakes and hulagirls tatooed on [arms and *deleted*] his [*inserted*] chest and I love you Rosie Probert on his belly, he roves with a herd of short-and-good-time cows in every naughty port and twines and souses with [the *deleted*] his [*inserted*] drowned and blowsy-breasted [dead *deleted*] ghosts [*inserted*]. He [cries as *deleted*] weeps as he sleeps & sails. *The entire passage deleted in ink.*

Followed by another manuscript draft in ink:

Captain Cat, at his window thrown wide to the sun and the old clippered seas of his long [gone *deleted*] dead [*inserted*] sailing, slumbers and voyages; ear-ringed and rolling, I Love You Rosie Probert tatooed on his belly, he brauls [*sic*] with broken bottles in the fug and babel of the dark *this unfinished passage deleted in ink.*

Followed by final manuscript draft in ink]

Captain Cat, at his window thrown wide to the sun

109

and the [long ago clippered seas, slumbers *deleted*]
clippered seas he sailed long ago when his eyes were
blue and bright, slumbers and voyages; ear-ringed
and rolling, I Love You Rosie Probert tatooed on his
belly, he brawls with broken bottles in the fug and
babel of the dark dock bars, roves with a herd of
short and good time cows in every naughty port and
twines and souses with the drowned and blowsy-
breasted dead. He weeps as he sleeps and sails. [*note
in margin*] Okay   MS
He weeps as he sleeps and sails, [*followed by line in
square brackets and note in round blackets*] [& the
tears run down his grog-blossomed nose.] (*not in
written versions* from sails on—)   N1

D 68, 20: ND 75, 19
SECOND VOICE
[*Omitted*]   M

D 68, 22–25: ND 75, 21–24
Lazy early Rosie with the flaxen thatch, whom he shared
with Tom-Fred the donkeyman and many another sea-
man, clearly and near to him speaks from the bedroom of
her dust.
    Lazy early Rosie with the flaxen thatch clearly and
    near to him speaks from the bedroom of her dust M

D 69, 28–29: ND 76, 28–77, 1
As true as I'm here
Dear you Tom Cat's tart
    As true as I'm here dear [*inserted*]
    [Dear *deleted*] You Tom Cat's tart   N1 N2
    As true as I'm here dear
    You Tom Cat's tart   M

D 70, 8–15: ND 76, 10–17
What seas were rocking [*to*] With my name on your belly
    [*Production note* more *deleted*]   MS
110

D 70, 27: ND 78, 1
At the door of my grave
    At the door of [the *deleted*] my grave   MS

D 71, 15–20: ND 78, 20–25
CHILD   Captain Cat is crying
FIRST VOICE   Captain Cat is crying
CAPTAIN CAT   Come back, come back,
    Child: Captain Cat is crying.
    1st Voice: Captain Cat is crying,   MS B2 M
    Captain Cat: Come back come back,   MS B2

D 71, 24–28: ND 79, 4–8
CHILD   He's crying all over his nose [*to*] down the street.
    [*Inserted in ink on typewritten page*]   MS

D 72, 4—73, 14: ND 79, 12–80, 24
She sees in the still middle of the bluebagged bay Nogood
Boyo fishing [*to*] **un**easy Eastern music undoes him in a
Japanese minute.
    [*Omitted*]   M

D 73, 12–13: ND 80, 22–23
through the warm white cloud where he lies,
    the warm white clouds   C

D 73, 27–28: ND 81, 13–14
Lazy she lies alone in clover and sweet-grass, seventeen
and never been sweet in the grass ho ho
    never been [sweet in the grass you liar *deleted*] sweet
    in the grass ho ho [*inserted in pencil*]   MS
    [*Omitted*]   M

D 74, 8–9: ND 81, 22–23
hang over him heavy as sheep
    heavy as [sleep *corrected to*] sheep   MS

D 74, 9–10: ND 81, 23–24
next to faint lady watercolours of pale green Milk Wood
like a lettuce salad dying.
    [*Deleted*]   N1 N2
    [*Omitted*]   M

D 74, 13: ND 81, 27
suffers in her stays.

    suffers in her stays [, and smiles *deleted*].   MS
    [*Transferred to* D 74, 11: ND 81, 25 *after* a pot in a
    palm,]   DA

D 74, 14–19: ND 82, 1–6
REV. ELI JENKINS Oh angels be careful there with your
knives and forks,
FIRST VOICE he prays. There is no known likeness of his
father Esau, who, undogcollared because of his little
weakness,

    Rev. Jenkins [*and*] *1st Voice* [*inserted in ink to turn*
    D 74, 15–16: ND 82, 2–3 *from narration into speech*]
            MS
    [*Rev. Eli Jenkins: to* he prays *deleted*]   N1 N2
    [*Rev. Eli Jenkins: to* he prays *omitted*]   M
    his father Esau who, undogcollared   MS

D 74, 20: ND 82, 7
was scythed to the bone one harvest by mistake
    was then scythed   C MS
    [then *deleted*]   N1 N2

D 75, 16–17: ND 83, 8–9
as he raves and dances among his summerbreathed slaves
    [summerbreathed *altered to*] summerbreath'd   N1
    summerbreath'd   M DA

D 75, 20–21: ND 83, 12–13
Bessie Bighead greets them by the names she gave them
when they were maidens.
    [*Inside the front cover of the folder containing the* MS
    was written an earlier draft of lines 20–25:
    Gwennie Bighead greets them by [name *deleted*] the
    names she has given them when they were maidens:
        Daisy, Buttercup,
        Peg, Meg, Buttercup, Moll

Fan from the Castle
[Shirley Liz *deleted*] & Daisy [Pearl *deleted*]
Theodosia]   MS cover
[Gwennie *deleted*] Bessie [*inserted*]   MS

D 76, 5–12: ND 83, 24–84, 4
the lock of hair of a first Lost Love. Conceived in Milk
Wood [*to*] and sleep until the night sucks out her soul
    the lock of hair of a first lost love.
    Rev. Eli Jenkins: Conceived in Milk Wood [*to*] and
    sleep
    Narrator: until the night   DA

D 76, 14–17: ND 84, 6–9
dusk showers slowly down over byre, sea and town.
    Utah Watkins curses through the farmyard on a
carthorse.
    [*No new paragraph for*] Utah Watkins   MS
    2nd Voice: [*inserted*] Utah Watkins   N1 N2
    2nd Voice: Utah Watkins   M

D 76, 20–21: ND 84, 12–13
FIRST VOICE   and the huge horse neighs softly
    [1st *deleted*] 2nd [*inserted*]   N1 N2
    2nd Voice: and the huge horse   M

D 76, 23: ND 84, 15
Now the town is dusk.
    1st Voice [*inserted*] Now the town is dusk.   N1 N2
    1st Voice: Now the town is dusk.   M

D 76, 23–78, 8: ND 84, 15–86, 8
Now the town is dusk [*to*] And then you must take them
off.
    [*Not in*]   C
    [*This section typed on separate sheet of paper, marked
    in pencil*]   Insert (A)   MS

D 76, 29–30: ND 84, 21–22
Mrs Ogmore-Pritchard, at the first drop of the dusk-shower, seals all her sea-view doors,
    seals all her Sea View doors,   MS—B2 M

D 77, 4–6: ND 84, 27–29
planning the loveless destruction of their glass widow, reluctantly sigh and sidle into her clean house.
    widow, reluctantly [*inserted*] sigh and sidle [with reluctance *deleted*] into her clean house.   MS

D 77, 16–78, 8: ND 85, 10–86, 8
MRS OGMORE-PRITCHARD Husbands, [*to*] And then you must take them off.
    [*Deleted*]   N1 N2
    [*Omitted*]   M

D 78, 9–22: ND 86, 9–22
SECOND VOICE Down in the dusking town, Mae Rose Cottage [*to*] the goats champ and sneer.
    [*Omitted*]   M

D 78, 11: ND 86, 11
listens to the nannygoats chew,
    [and listening *deleted*] listens [*inserted*]   MS
    [listens *deleted*] listening [*inserted*]   N1 N2

D 78, 11–12: ND 86, 12
draws circles of lipstick round her nipples.
    [*Omitted*]   A

D 78, 22: ND 86, 22
the goats champ and sneer.
    [*Note in margin*] Insert A & B [& C *deleted*]   MS

D 78, 23–79, 7: ND 86, 23–87, 17
FIRST VOICE And at the doorway of Bethesda House [*to*] And say, good-bye—but just for now.
    [*Not in*]   C
    [*This section is in D.T.'s hand, on two pages torn from*
114

exercise book, numbered 16 and 17 deleted, headed]
A [*The Reverend Eli Jenkins's Sunset Poem deleted*]
MS

D 78, 23–24: ND 86, 23–24
FIRST VOICE   And at the doorway
    [*1st Voice omitted*]   MS
    1st [*deleted and then restored*] *Voice:*   N1
    2nd *Voice:*   M

D 78, 24–25: ND 86, 24–26
And at the doorway of Bethesda House, the Reverend
Jenkins recites to Llaregyb Hill his sunset poem,
    and [*inserted*] At the doorway of Bethesda House,
    the Reverend Jenkins recites to [the tall *deleted*]
    Llareggub Hill his sunset poem.   MS

D 79, 2: ND 87, 2
Every morning when I wake,
    Every morning, when I wake,   MS

D 79, 3: ND 87, 3
Dear Lord, a little prayer I make,
    Dear Lord a little prayer I make, ·   MS B2

D 79, 14–17: ND 87, 14–17
O let us see another day!
Bless us this night, I pray,
And to the sun we all will bow
And say, good-bye—but just for now!
    [Look mercifully down, I pray,
    And let us love thee in our way *deleted*]
    [*inserted page*] B
    [Bless us this holy [long dark *inserted and deleted*]
      winding night, I pray,
    And let us see another day,
    [Then safe in thy dear arms I vow
    We'll tell the sun—Goodbye, for now *deleted*]

115

O let us see another day!
Bless us this winding night, I pray,
[So *deleted*] And [*inserted*] to the [great *added above
line*] sun we all [may *deleted*] will [*inserted*] bow
And say, Dear Sir, Goodbye—for now.
And say Goodbye [*deleted and restored*]—but just
    for now.
The entire passage deleted in pencil and ink]

O let us see another day!
Bless us this [winding *deleted*] night, I pray,
And to the sun we all will bow
And say, Goodbye—but just for now!   MS

Bless us this holy [*inserted*] night, I pray   N1
Bless us this holy night, I pray,   B2 M
[*Footnote on* 'holy' *and* 'winding']   DA

D 79, 17: ND 87, 17
And say, good-bye—but just for now!
And say, Good-bye—but just for now!   MS
[*End of inserted page* B]
And say [, *deleted*] goodbye—   N1 N2

D 79, 18–19: ND 87, 18–19
FIRST VOICE   Jack Black prepares once more
[*Typescript resumes here*]   MS
[*1st deleted: 2nd inserted and deleted*] *1st* [*restored*]
                                                        N1

    2nd Voice: M

D 79, 26–81, 2: ND 88, 1–89 8
SECOND VOICE   And Lily Smalls is up to Nogood Boyo
[*to*] . . . oh, Gossamer, open yours!
    [*Omitted*]   M

D 79, 26–28: ND 88, 1–3
SECOND VOICE   And Lily Smalls is up to Nogood Boyo in
the washhouse.
    [*Not in*]   C

116

Add 2nd Voice: And Lily Smalls is up to nogood
Boyo in the washhouse. [*Inserted in pencil*]   MS

D 80, 2: ND 88, 5
And Cherry Owen, sober as Sunday
    Cherry Owens [*sic throughout this sequence to* D 80,
    22: ND 89, 1]   MS
    [And *deleted*] Cherry Owen [s *deleted: sic to* D 80, 22:
    ND 89, 1]   N1 N2

D 80, 14–15: ND 88, 17–18
And aren't I a lucky woman? Because I love them both.
    [*Production note*] slower   MS

D 80, 16–81, 2: ND 88, 19–89, 8
SINBAD   Evening, Cherry [*to*] . . . oh, Gossamer, open
yours!
    [*Not in*]   C
    [*typed on separate slip of paper, pasted to foot of p. 49
    of* MS, *marked*] Insert B   MS

D 80, 25: ND 89, 4
The Sailors Arms is always open.
    The *Sailors* Arms is always open,   MS
    The Sailors' Arms is always open,   B1—B2

D 81, 1–2: ND 89, 7–8
SINBAD   . . . oh, Gossamer, open yours!
    Oh, Gossamer, open yours!   MS B1 N2 B2
    [*Sinbad*: Oh, Gossamer, open yours! *deleted*:
    followed by * Insert *deleted: and by last line of page
    67 of* B1 *2nd Voice:* Mr Waldo in his corner of the
    Sailors' Arms, sings: *deleted*] *Sinbad:* Oh, Gossamer,
    open yours! [*at top of p. 67A of* N1]   N1

* *This asterisk does not refer to footnote, but was
written by D.T.*

D 81, 3–82, 27: ND 89, 9–91, 8
FIRST VOICE   Dusk is drowned for ever [*to*] made them-
selves a wife out of flowers.
   [*This sequence* [1] *not in*]   C MS B1
   [*Printed in Footnote*]   DA

D 81, 6: ND 89, 12
and from the larrupped waves the lights of the lamps
   larrupped waves, the lights   N1 N2 B2 M

D 81, 13: ND 89, 19
SECOND WOMAN'S VOICE (*Singing*)
   2nd Woman's Voice: [*not singing*]   N1 N2 B2 M

D 81, 13–17: ND 89, 19–23
SECOND WOMAN'S VOICE [*to*] Down will come grandpa,
whiskers and all.
   [*Omitted*]   A

D 81, 19–20: ND 89, 25–26
or their daughters cover up the old unwinking men like
parrots,
   cover up [*up omitted in typescript, inserted by D.T.*]
                                        N1

D 81, 28: ND 90, 8
Accordion music: dim
   Accordian [*sic throughout in* N1 N2] music—dim
                                    N1 N2
   Accordion music—dim   B2 M
   [*Accordion music omitted throughout*]   A

---

[1] *This sequence was written by D.T. in New York before
the final stage-readings in October, 1953. A typescript was
sent by Ruthven Todd to D.C., and was incorporated in* B2
and (except for Mr Waldo's song) in A. *The text was
subsequently confirmed by a photostat of* N1, *in which the
extra material had been inserted, and by* M. *The script of*
B2 *containing this sequence was not a carbon copy of* N1,
but was separately typed.

D 82, 5: ND 90, 13
Accordion music louder, then fading under
   Accordion music up and down and continuing dim
                          N1 N2 B2 M

D 82, 9: ND 90, 17
A DRINKER
   1st Drinker: N1 N2 B2 M

D 82, 11: ND 90, 19
CHERRY OWEN
   2nd Drinker: N1 N2 B2 M

D 82, 14–15: ND 90, 22–23
righteously says Cherry Owen who has just downed
seventeen pints
   righteously says a drinker who has   M

D 82, 19: ND 90, 28
Accordion music fades into silence
   [*Not in*]   N1 N2 B2 M

D 82, 20–24: ND 91, 1–5
FIRST VOICE Llaregyb Hill, writes the Reverend Jenkins
in his poem-room,
REV. ELI JENKINS Llaregyb Hill, that mystic tumulus,
   Llareggub Hill, writes the Reverend Jenkins in his
   poem-room, that mystic tumulus   N1 N2 M
   in his poem-room,
   Rev. Eli Jenkins: Llareggub Hill, [*inserted by D.C.*
   for B.B.C. production] that mystic tumulus, B2 A

D 82, 26–27: ND 91, 7–8
where the old wizards made themselves a wife out of
flowers.
   [*Followed by sound effect*] *Accordion music out*
                          N1 N2 B2 M
   [*End of inserted typescript*]   N1 N2
   [*Top of p. 50 of typescript of* MS *is marked*] Insert C
                              MS

D 82, 29–83, 31: ND 91, 9–92, 13
SECOND VOICE Mr Waldo, in his corner of the Sailors
Arms, sings: [*to*] Bring along your chimbley brush!
  [*Not in*]   C
  [*This section is in D.T.'s hand, on a page torn from an
  exercise book, numbered 3 deleted, headed*] C Mr
  Waldo's Song   MS
  [*Omitted*]   A M

D 82, 29: ND 91, 9
SECOND VOICE
  [*No attribution to 1st or 2nd Voice*]   MS
  2nd Voice: [*inserted*]   B1

D 83, 6: ND 91, 17
Six cold pennies he gave me
  Six [small *deleted*] cold [*inserted*] pennies   MS

D 83, 15: ND 91, 26
To live so cruel cheap
  To live so [cold & *deleted*] cruel [*inserted*] cheap MS

After D 83, 17: ND 91, 28
And liquor that makes you weep?
  [*Insertion mark in margin, with note*] more [*i.e. more
  lines to be added*]   MS

D 83, 23: ND 92, 5
Black as the ace of spades
  Black as [a blackamoor *deleted*] the ace of spades
  [*inserted*]   MS

D 83, 24: ND 92, 6
O nobody's swept my chimbley
  Oh [*added in margin*] Nobody's swept my chimbley
                                                                  MS

D 83, 25: ND 92, 7
Since my husband went his ways.
  Since my husband [went to war *deleted*] went [away
  deleted] his ways   MS
120

After D 83, 31: ND 92, 13
Bring along your chimbley brush!
    [Sweep sweep chimbley sweep
    I cried through Pembroke City
    And soon a score of kind young women
    Took me in from pity
    Poor little chimbley sweep they said
    Black as a blackamoor
    Are you as nice at chimneys
    As [Bethig *altered to*] Betty the Duckpond swore
    The entire passage deleted in ink]   MS
    [*On verso*] More Stuff for Actors to say [*see p.* 36] MS

D 84, 1–85, 7: ND 92, 14–92, 20
FIRST VOICE Blind Captain Cat climbs into his bunk [*to*]
Cherry Owen who is resting on the tombstone on his way
home.
    [*Not in*]   C

D 84, 3–4: ND 92, 16–17
Through the voyages of his tears he sails to see the dead.
    of his tears, he sails   MS—B2 M ND

D 84, 19–20: ND 93, 5–6
SECOND VOICE Listen to the night breaking
    [*Deleted*]   N1 N2
    [*Omitted*]   M

D 84, 21–22: ND 93, 7–8
FIRST VOICE Organ Morgan goes to chapel to play the
organ.
    [*1st deleted*] *2nd* [*inserted*]   N1
    2nd Voice: M

D 84, 23: ND 93, 9
He sees Bach lying on a tombstone.
    on a tombstone. [*Followed by manuscript insertion*]

He plays alone at night to anyone who will listen:
lovers, revellers, the silent dead, tramps or sheep.

                                                          N1 N2

He plays alone [*as in* N1, *to*] tramps or sheep.   N3 B1 M

[*This passage omitted*]   A

[*This passage printed in Footnote*]   DA

D 84, 24–85, 7: ND 93, 10–20

ORGAN MORGAN   Johann Sebastian! [*to*] resting on the
tombstone on his way home.

[*Omitted*]   M

D 84, 26–27: ND 93, 12–13

CHERRY OWEN (*Drunkenly*) Who?

[*Production note*] Drunker   N1

D 85, 1–2: ND 93, 14–15

ORGAN MORGAN   Johann Sebastian mighty Bach. Oh
Bach fach.[1]

    Oh, Bach, fach.   MS—B2

    Oh Bachfach.   ND

D 85, 6–7: ND 93, 19–20

says Cherry Owen who is resting on the tombstone on his
way home.

[*Omitted*]   DA

D 85, 8–10: ND 93, 21–23

happily apart from one another at the top and the sea-
end of the town

    at the top [*of deleted*] and [*inserted*] the sea-end   MS

D 85, 11: ND 93, 24

In the warm White Book of Llaregyb you will find

    of Llareggub [*inserted in pencil*] you will find   MS

---

[1] *The Welsh word for 'little' (as a term of endearment)
is 'bach' in the masculine gender, 'fach' in the feminine:
pronounced as in 'Bach'.*

D 85, 12–22: ND 94, 1–12
the little maps of the islands of their contentment [*to*] he
hugs his lovely money to his own heart.

    the islands of their contentment. [*The following
insertions and deletions are in pencil, altering the
typescript narration into dialogue*]
    Myfanwy [*inserted*] Oh, my Mog, I am yours forever
[writes Miss Myfanwy Price *deleted*]
    1st Voice [*inserted*] and [*altered to*] And she [*inserted*]
looks around with pleasure [*to*] never enter.
    Mog [*inserted*] Come to my arms, Myfanwy [cries
Mr Edwards *deleted*] And he [he *inserted*] hugs his
lovely money [. *deleted*] to his *own* heart. [*inserted*]
    [*All insertions in pencil*]   MS

D 85, 23–24: ND 94, 13–14
And Mr Waldo drunk in the dusky wood hugs his lovely
Polly Garter

    drunk in [the dusky wood *altered to*] Milk Wood
                                      N1 N2
    drunk in Milk Wood   M

D 85, 24–25: ND 94, 14–15
rattling tongues of the neighbours and the birds,
    the [*inserted in pencil*] birds,   MS

D 85, 27–29: ND 94, 17–19
But it is not *his* name that Polly Garter whispers as she
lies under the oak [1] and loves him back. Six feet deep that
name sings in the cold earth.
    [*Production note*] softer   MS
    [*Production note* for that name sings: *heavy under-
lining below* name]   MS

D 86, 11–12: ND 95, 3–4
the fairday farmhands' wantoning ignorant chapel of
bridesbeds,
    chapel of bridebeds,   C MS

---

[1] *Compare 'Lie still under the oak' at the close of David
Jones'* In Parenthesis (*see p. 10*).

D 86, 13–14: ND 95, 5–6
a greenleaved sermon on the innocence of men,
    a greenleaved sermon [to *deleted*] on [*inserted*] the
    innocence of men,   MS

D 86, 15: ND 95, 7–8
this one Spring day.
    this one [one *inserted*] spring day.   MS
    this one [s *altered to* S] Spring day.   N1 N2